laity must be educated to educate and new forms of liturgy and worship must call for increased congregational participation.

Representative resources are:

Hymnal for Juniors in Worship and Study, edited by the late W. Lawrence Curry, which explores hymnody at the junior church school age level. *Let's Sing Together* with its companion record of the same title and the forthcoming *Worship and Hymns for All Occasions* book-and-record duo are just two among many teaching helps aimed at a special age group.

Liturgy Coming to Life, by John A. T. Robinson, author of the controversy-causing *Honest to God,* suggests changes in worship forms. In *Life Without Living: People of the Inner City,* James A. Gittings, a newspaperman, uses his reportorial flair to apprise laymen and educators alike of the inner-city mission of the church. In *Straight Talk About Teaching in Today's Church,* Locke E. Bowman, Jr., Teacher-in-Residence with The Arizona Experiment in Biblical Studies and Teaching, takes his readers right to the church classroom " scene of action." *Let's Talk About God: Devotions for Families with Young Children* declares itself by title to be a constantly used resource for parents who want the instruction they give their children to be based on Christian principles, and its ex-social worker author, Gertrude Ann Priester, speaks from a wealth of firsthand experience gained as a children's editor for a church publishing house.

Dr. Cully's latest book joins these distinguished education aids and, predictably, will become a Christian education basic, as have her *Children in the Church, Imparting the Word: The Bible in Christian Education,* and *An Introductory Theological Wordbook,* which she wrote in collaboration with her noted educator-husband, Kendig Brubaker Cully (*see back of jacket*).

DR. IRIS V. CULLY is a graduate of The Hartford Seminary Foundation, Garrett Theological Seminary, and Northwestern University (Ph.D.). She is Associate Professor of Christian Education, Yale Divinity School.

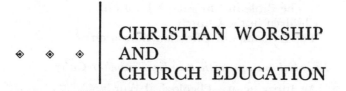

CHRISTIAN WORSHIP AND CHURCH EDUCATION

CHRISTIAN WORSHIP AND CHURCH EDUCATION

by IRIS V. CULLY

THE WESTMINSTER PRESS
Philadelphia

Published by The Westminster Press®
Philadelphia, Pennsylvania

PRINTED IN THE UNITED STATES OF AMERICA

71174

CONTENTS

CONTENTS

◈ ◈ ◈ PREFACE

I F THE CONTINUOUS OUTPUT of books on the subject is any
indication, renewal of worship is an engrossing concern
of the Christian community. Newly developed orders for
Sunday worship have been issued by several denominations
in response to this stimulus. No one yet knows the extent to
which the congregations will accept the practical results of
these reformulations where they have any option. The familiar casts a binding spell, and American churches have
not been notable for educating their members in the understanding of worship.

To assist in the amelioration of this lack is the purpose
of this book. The background for the present interest in
worship is recounted for the benefit of those in religious
education who understandably have not had time to become widely familiar in every field contiguous to their
own. The Biblical and historical development of Christian
worship is the rationale for a generally agreed upon form
and similarity of content which characterize Christian liturgies. Understanding the psychological factors that encourage or impede participation in worship and the sociological
factors that influence the development of worshiping congregations is necessary in order to assess the meaning of
worship for the participants. Succeeding chapters explore

the content materials of worship: Scripture, preaching, prayer, and music. The Lord's Supper, so central to the expression of Christian worship, is examined as a concrete manner of communication. Some examples of the wealth of symbolic modes, known by speech, sight, or action, are brought together in one chapter. The book closes with an emphasis on the meaning of worship as the way by which the questions of life find answers and through which Christians are strengthened for their daily life in God's service.

Some may be surprised that just one chapter is given to the subject of church school worship. This subject has been helpfully treated in a practical book by Paul H. Vieth, my distinguished emeritus colleague at The Divinity School, Yale University, and needs no repetition. In it church school worship is placed in relation to the worship of the whole church.

The writer believes that this is the stance from which those responsible for church school education must view worship. The neglect of this proportional view has too often resulted in parallel structures for church school worship and an ever-increasing delay in introducing young people to the whole worshiping community.

For this reason, in addition to being a source of quick reference for religious educators (lay and clerical — which includes just about everybody), the present book hopes to make clear the educational implications of worship. For centuries, most religious education was accomplished through participation in the liturgy. American Protestants, particularly in urban and suburban settings, have operated outside this base for only two generations — less than a century. It should not be too difficult to move again into the mainstream of Christian practice.

The Report of the Theological Commission on Worship of the World Council of Churches, *Faith and Order Findings*. Paper No. 39 (Augsburg Publishing House, 1963), p. 23, recommended the following:

Instruction of the young in worship within an ecumenical context.

The setting up of study groups for liturgical questions.

Visits by local congregations to the normal worship of other congregations.

Individual or group visits to other churches when traveling abroad.

People learn through the liturgy: words and action bear the message to those who are involved through participation. Opportunities to understand occur during and after the service, in educational groups such as classes, or at home. Ministers and other educators need to become more aware of this primary resource.

While this book was in the final stages of thinking and writing, the author was helped by the stimulus of her students in a seminar at Yale which explored these areas. Thanks go to David Abbott, Douglas Farnhill, David L. Jones, Joseph Lin, John O'Neill, Ronald Ray, and Donald Stauffer.

Husband Kendig Brubaker Cully raised questions, corrected copy, and provided the security of love which makes the struggle to produce possible. His approval brings the joy in accomplishment.

I. V. C.

The Divinity School
Yale University
New Haven, Connecticut

CHAPTER 1 | # THE SERVICE
OF WORSHIP

WORSHIP IS CENTRAL in the Christian community, and participation in congregational worship is one of the marks of the Christian person. The word "liturgy" means "common work" and suggests an act in which all present are engaged. The phrase "church service" similarly suggests mutual action.

There are varied modes of action. The person who listens enthralled to a symphony performance or who watches intently the unfolding of a play is engaged in activity that can hardly be called passive. Nevertheless, this action could be carried on without his presence, as indeed is done at a recording session or a taping for television. Can Christian worship be carried on similarly? This has happened: the Roman rite has interpreted "congregation" to mean the server assisting at Mass, but today questions are being raised at this point. Protestant ministers and congregations have been known to feel awkward when the assemblage was small.

There is increasingly in all Christendom an awareness that the real meaning of liturgy, namely, "service," is not realized when there is a pronounced difference between the work of the leader (clergyman) and that of the congregation. A congregation cannot be an audience or an assemblage of spectators whose participation is primarily that of watching and listening. A mutuality is called for, so that all present become necessary to the completion of the work, and the part of each is dependent upon the part of the others.

Christian worship is not a gathering together for mutual encouragement, although this may result, or for individual illumination and/or comfort, which could also happen. Christian worship occurs because God dwells among his people through this means. At the heart of the service are the words, " Where two or three are gathered in my name, there am I in the midst of them " (Matt. 18:20) . This precludes a decision to stay away because the minister might be dull, the choir feeble, or the congregation small, the inference being that one could worship "better" at home. Christians gather to rejoice together with their Lord, whom they know has come among them in a special way through this event.

WORSHIP IN THE NEW TESTAMENT

The Acts of the Apostles opens with the last appearance of the risen Christ to his followers, when he commanded them to wait in Jerusalem until the Holy Spirit came among them. They were continually in the Temple blessing God, and ten days later were together in one place when they were filled with the Holy Spirit. After that day " they devoted themselves to the apostles' teaching and fellowship, to the breaking of bread and the prayers " (Acts 2:42) . There are not enough references to worship in the New Testament to make it possible to reconstruct the form(s) of service. Acts 2:46; 5:42; 20:7; 27:35 f. suggest preaching, prayer, and the breaking of bread, while I Cor., chs. 11 and 14, suggest the conduct of worship in general and ch. 11 the Lord's Supper in particular. Elements of primitive Christian worship may be discerned in parts of

Revelation, and materials from the early service may be found there.

The apostle Paul addressed First Corinthians to a church gathered for worship:

> To the church of God which is at Corinth, to those sanctified in Christ Jesus, called to be saints together with all those who in every place call on the name of our Lord Jesus Christ, both their Lord and ours:
> Grace to you and peace from God our Father and the Lord Jesus Christ.

Such a greeting may have been the customary opening for a service.[1] (Cf. Rom. 1:7; Rev. 1:4.) This is often followed by a prayer of thanksgiving — for the steadfastness of the church, for the grace given them — and a petition that they may continue to grow in the gospel. Sometimes there follows an affirmation of the gospel (Col. 1:13 ff.; Phil. 2:5-11) in a rhythmic form, suggesting that early hymns or poems in praise of God's redeeming work in Christ were already being used in worship. The " preaching " follows in two sections: the doctrinal and the practical. The letters end with a " Grace be with you " (Col. 4:18), or " The grace of the Lord Jesus Christ be with your spirit " (Phil. 4:23), or a similar blessing.

Echoes of forms used in the earliest worship of the church are found in the triadic formula: Father, Son, Spirit — or God, Jesus, Spirit (I Cor. 12:4-6; Eph. 4:4-6). These are not theological speculations, but affirmations of believers, assured that their gathering in worship was blessed by the Spirit, sent of God, and made known in Christ. In this lay the awesome excitement of worship.

Many expressions of praise are found in the forms of doxology (To him be glory) and eulogy (Praised be . . .): Rom. 9:5b; I Tim. 1:17 (" To the King of ages, immortal, invisible, the only God, be honor and glory for ever and ever. Amen ") ; I Peter 4:11. Usually this expression is a conclusion to a greeting, to a section of the writing, or to a whole letter. The fact that it stands apart suggests a form commonly used in worship which both writer and hearers would recognize. (Phil. 4:20; Heb. 13:20 f.; Rev. 1:4b-5.) Seemingly, a reading or message was usually rounded off with a doxology and the people replied, " Amen," thus making it their own and affirming their participation in what was said. In effect, this was saying that Christians glorified God by their lives and that the ways of Christian living, of which the messages spoke, were the acting out of what God had done for them in Jesus Christ. When each gave money for a collection to a sister church in need, this too was a way of glorifying God. (II Cor. 9:13.)

The song of the angels (Luke 2:14) and the song of the pilgrims at Jerusalem (Luke 19:38) are early hymns of praise, but where they were originally used in the service is not known. " Blessed be God " is a phrase coming from Hebrew worship, which occurs sometimes at the beginning of a letter in thanksgiving for churches or following the grace (II Cor. 1:3; I Peter 1:3; Eph. 1:3) .

Several phrases in Aramaic have come into the Greek manuscripts. Such is *Maranatha,* meaning " The Lord has come," or " Come, Lord " (I Cor. 16:22) , both the affirmation of the people of Christ that he has come and the prayer that he will return. *Abba* is the utterance given to Christians to say because the Spirit has made them children of God (Rom. 8:15 f.; Gal. 4:6) . " Amen " is a cry from Hebrew worship giving assent to words spoken. In the New Testament epistles it occurs commonly as a response to prayer.

Finally, there is the concluding grace affixed to each letter, apparently an ending to worship: " The grace of the Lord Jesus be with you " (I Cor. 16:23) .

Baptism was accompanied by an affirmation of faith, " Christ is Lord," but it is not known to what extent a confession of this type may have been used in the worship of the community. This might be a spontaneous cry of joy rather than a regularly used form. There are also hymnlike passages, confessional in form, which may have been used more regularly: I Peter 3:18-20 and Eph. 1:17-22 speak of God's mighty acts. Col. 3:16 speaks of singing " psalms and hymns and spiritual songs with thankfulness in your hearts to God." There may be little difference among these. They were in praise of God, an expression of thanksgiving to him, inspired by the Spirit and offered in the name of Jesus. This feeling made Christian hymns new and different from all others, as the writer of Revelation notes in quoting such a hymn (chs. 5:9 f.; 14:3). Other hymns of praise to Christ are found in I Tim. 3:16 and Phil. 2:5-11. These are quoted as passages already known to the hearers of the letters, and were probably familiar materials of worship. Mention also should be made of psalm hymns incorporated into the early chapters of Luke's Gospel which have persisted in the church's worship and which show similarities to Jewish psalms: the song of Simeon (ch. 2:29-32), the song of Mary (ch. 1:46-55), and Zechariah's song (ch. 1:68-79).

The earliest Jewish Christians attended the synagogue service and there heard the Law and the Prophets read. Nothing in the New Testament suggests that Old Testament passages were a part of Christian worship. Paul had written that Christians were freed from the Law. Possibly only Christian writings were read aloud, and this could explain the arrangement of the Gospels in sections, the grouping of stories around key words, and the stylized accounts of the passion. The apostle Paul wrote more than once of receiving and handing down the Christian tradition. He expected his letters to be read aloud in the congregation, and this seems also to have been the intent of the writer of Revelation. The Gospels arose out of such oral traditions. Preaching in the early church was a form of glad witness to what God had done, the recounting of his action, and the affirmation that the Spirit works in the church for its upbuilding.

In the church, prayer was made in the name of Jesus. The prayer of the congregation had a special importance: " If you ask anything of the Father, he will give it you in my name. Hitherto you have asked nothing in my name; ask, and you will receive, that your joy may be full " (John 16:23-24). Jesus himself in significant moments, as at the transfiguration and in Gethsemane, took three disciples with him. The Lord's Prayer was intended to be used by the congregation: it was given to the disciples (Matt. 5:1; 6:9-13; Luke 11:1-4); it is set in plural form, and the concerns are communal as well as personal. Paul asks his congregation to pray for him (Col. 4:3; I Thess. 5:25; II Thess. 3:1). Even when one is praying alone, all are linked in the thought that someone elsewhere is engaged in prayer. Their confidence is based on what God has done. When Peter and John were released from prison and found their way to where their fellow Christians were gathered, they " lifted their voices together to God " in a prayer of thanksgiving, which in its formal character suggests a form of early worship (Acts 4:24 ff.). They affirm God's saving work and pray that they may witness boldly.

The relation of God to Jesus in primitive Christian prayer is put this way by Gerhard Delling:

> The whole evidence seems not unimportant for reaching a judgment about the place of Jesus in primitive Christian Worship. Christ was its actual content; confession of faith in *Him* played a decisive part; hymns praised the salvation which was wrought through *Him;* the burning expectation of the Church looked out for *Him.* Through *Him* the old man was overcome; in *Him* the new being was bestowed; " in *Him* " the common fellowship was founded. *He* was present in the Lord's Supper; *His* Spirit furnished the utterances in the life of Worship; " in *His* Name " men called upon God in thanks and requests.

Yet, for all that, it remained God who had provided salvation; God who carries out the plan of salvation-history; God toward whom the consummation flows; God from whom the call went forth; God for whom the Church is being built as a temple; God whose rule is the goal of all services of Worship. The Lordship of Jesus took nothing from the power of God, but was only the manifestation of the divine glory.[2]

Primitive Christian worship included the " breaking of bread," which represented the last meal that the disciples shared with their Lord before his passion, witnessing to this in the present and looking toward his return. The familiar phrase " break bread " and the accompanying gesture are found often in the New Testament: during the feeding of the multitude (told in all four Gospels), the supper at Emmaus, a meal by the shore of the lake — all times when Christ appears among his own. The phrase is also used in Acts 20:7 when the apostle Paul meets the gathering at Troas. In this action the church recalls an event, participates in the death and resurrection of the Lord, and rejoices in being part of his Kingdom. The people bring their gifts; they say amen to the thanksgiving and the blessing; they eat and drink; they are sent forth as witnesses.

This illustrates the corporate quality of Christian worship. The deep level of fellowship resides here — not in solitariness, but where two or three are gathered or where thousands come. The Lord's Supper is the climax of congregational worship — a celebration, a joyous event, a meaning best conveyed by the term " Eucharist," or " thanksgiving." The presence of the Holy Spirit brought excitement to the hearing of the story of salvation, the utterance of their petitions, and the singing of their psalms of praise. The presence of Christ at the Supper brought unspeakable joy to his people, assurance that they were partakers in his eternal life.

THE DEVELOPMENT OF CHRISTIAN WORSHIP

References to Christian worship occur briefly in second-century writings. Ignatius in several of his letters mentions the celebration of the Lord's Supper. The Didache outlines a prayer of thanksgiving, and in another place has a rather full description of what is more probably a love feast. The prayer of thanksgiving and consecration was a " free " prayer during the first century or so, but soon became stylized in terms of what it would include: the recital of the event, the blessing of the bread and wine, and the thanksgiving. This was followed by the breaking of the bread and its distribution to the whole congregation by the elders and deacons.[3] The first reference to Christian worship from a non-Christian source is found in a letter which Pliny wrote to the Emperor Trajan, mentioning the Sunday gathering for the breaking of bread. The first explanation known to have been given by a Christian to the non-Christian world is made by Justin the Martyr in his *Apology* (c. 155) :

On the day which is called Sunday, all who live in the cities or in the countryside gather together in one place. And the memoirs of the apostles or the writings of the prophets are read as long as there is time. Then, when the reader has finished, the president, in a discourse, admonishes and invites the people to practice these examples of virtue. Then we all stand up together and offer prayers. And, as we mentioned before, when we have finished the prayer, bread is presented, and wine with water; the president likewise offers up prayers and thanksgivings according to his ability, and the people assent by saying " amen." The elements which have been " eucharistized " are distributed and received by each one; and they are sent to the absent by the deacons. Those who are prosperous, if they wish, contribute what each one deems appropriate; and the collection is deposited with the president; and he takes care . . . of the needy.[4]

The prayers and thanksgivings are given a suggested form in the Apostolic Tradition of Hippolytus, written about 200. Descriptions of the service are also to be found in the First Letter of Clement, and the writings of Tertullian. The first complete liturgies so far discovered are contained in the Euchologion (prayer book) of Serapion, Bishop of Thmuis in the Nile delta in the fourth century, and the Apostolic Constitutions from the same period.

The form of the Western rite was complete by the fifth century, and became known as the Mass, from the concluding words of dismissal, *Ite, missa est,* the blessing and sending forth of the worshiping congregation. Three books of liturgy have been found, dating from about the fifth to the seventh century: the Leonine, Gelasian, and Gregorian Sacramentaries. They indicate action, movement, color, and participation by many groups in the service: clergy, assistants, choir, people. Through succeeding centuries changes were made, incorporating into one uniform rite some of the elaboration used in the Gallican rite familiar in northern Europe.

The uniformity was broken in the sixteenth century. Each of the Reformers developed a rite. Some were closer to the Roman rite (Luther, Cranmer), some were midway (Strasbourg — Bucer, Geneva — Calvin), some radical (Zwingli, the Anabaptist groups). The Council of Trent appointed a commission to try to bring the Roman rite back to its pre-Gallican form, and some simplification was made. Succeeding centuries saw the development of orders for Sunday worship in the Church of Scotland and later among the Methodists. While the founders of these movements urged a return to participation in the Eucharistic rite, the people, long used to receiving the Communion annually, refused. Morning prayer, derived from the monastic offices of the hours, and ante-Communion, the so-called service of the catechumens preceding the Eucharistic service, became normative forms for Protestant worship. Roman Catholics continued to assist at Mass by their presence but to receive Communion infrequently.

For the first thousand years after Christ the altar table had been central, the celebrants standing around it; but in the Gothic period, when the people's participation often became little more than observation, the table was set against the wall and the celebrant offered the sacrifice of praise and thanksgiving in behalf of the people while facing the altar in the same direction as they did. Lutherans and Anglicans continued this practice (except for a period in the Church of England when the table was placed forward), but in Calvinist tradition the pulpit became central, high and lifted up, and the table was placed beneath it, on a level with the people.

Liturgical reformulation and rethinking is one of the major areas of ferment within Western Christendom today. The Vatican Council II has returned the liturgy (which was Latin for centuries) to the vernacular and emphasized an active participation of the people, whose responses and amens are essential. Laymen now read the lessons, and the Eucharistic elements are brought forward with other gifts for the offertory. The procession of the Gospel book highlights the reading from the words of the Lord; sermons are prepared with new seriousness; the singing of hymns during the Communion accentuates the communal act of worship rather than the element of personal devotion. These emphases, along with the essential brevity of the service, make it an effective avenue of corporate worship for people from all sociocultural backgrounds. Change is not easy: everyone clings to the familiar. Both clergy and people have sometimes been resistant, while others have enthusiastically welcomed the clarity now given to the rite.

Protestants are in the same situation, and react similarly. Several large denominations have issued provisional orders of worship,[5] which try to recover the essential features of the Western rite as it developed across the first few cen-

turies. Basically, this consists of the service of the Word —
the teaching service in which the baptized and the learners
participated in the early church — which leads up to the
Eucharistic service. Weekly use of the latter is encouraged
but far from being realized. Kierkegaard's much-quoted
simile is coming to fruition as congregations take seriously
his insight that the minister is the prompter, they are the
actors, while God is the audience.

Nineteenth-century curiosity about origins is partly responsible. Along with discovering early Biblical texts,
archaeologists began collecting the writings of the church
fathers, Biblical commentaries, and theological treatises.
Today the few ancient liturgical writings available make it
clear that the forms of worship used in the apostolic church
are not as recoverable as the founders of some reform
groups had imagined. The method of form criticism —
attempting to find out the situations which produced the
various New Testament writings — has suggested the possibility that liturgical fragments are present. Scholars are
now trying to decipher which materials might have been
used in worship and which in teaching, as well as what
kinds of assemblages called forth these readings. Nobody
today feels sure of defining the various orders and functions in the primitive church. If we are not so literal as to
appoint exorcists or to allow speaking in tongues, perhaps
we should also be more flexible about other practices that
we have thought were " early church." What is wrong with
additions? When is an addition enrichment and when dis-
tortion? When is it helpful to use original materials, and
when is it useful to be contemporary? These are some of
the questions leading to a renewed understanding of the
meaning of the church's worship.

The World Council of Churches has been responsible
for much of the ferment among Protestant groups. The
book *Ways of Worship,* published in 1951, brought together the divergent viewpoints of separate articles. The

latest sequel, an aftermath of the Third Assembly in 1963, is a revealing document of what has been happening in a decade.[6] Books in popular style have been written from within several denominations to explain the attempt to recover both the formulations of the sixteenth century and new-found understandings of earlier patterns of worship.[7]

A Swiss Reformed theologian, Jean-Jacques von Allmen, says:

> A Church reformation which would stop short of a liturgical reformation, and miss the means of concrete expression which this affords, would sterilize the Word of God instead of allowing it to bear its fruit. And for this reason I do not think it an exaggeration to say that if the Biblical renascence which our time has witnessed is reluctant and afraid to engage in the immense task of a liturgical reform, it will turn to our condemnation. It is not a better catechesis, nor a reorganization of the Church, nor a new awareness of the appeal sounded in our ears by the weary and the heavy-laden — it is not these things which will justify the Church of our time: it is a liturgical reform because it is this which will justify in its repercussions this catechesis, this reorganization, this diaconate inasmuch as it will prevent them from degenerating into a Biblicist intellectualism, an Erastian legalism or a socialistic activism.[8]

THE FORM OF WORSHIP

The service of the Word is essentially a teaching service, and was that part of Christian worship in which, during the early centuries, the learners, or catechumens, not yet baptized, were present. It opens with a greeting, such as the apostle writes, " Grace be with you." Today this finds form in the opening sentences or call to worship. The ancient versicles, " The Lord be with you," and the reply, " And with you too," are a reminder that the worship of the church is mutually engaged in by the one who presides and the rest of the congregation. The opening when in prayer form acknowledges with thanksgiving the presence of the Holy Spirit among his people as they gather, obedient to the command, and in expectation of his blessing upon their common service. An opening hymn of praise, common today, reflects this same purpose. The Kyrie eleison (Lord, have mercy upon us) is also, in its original intention, an ascription of praise, reminiscent of the greeting to the emperor as the merciful one. The Gloria in Excelsis, incorporating the hymn of the angels at the Nativity (and reflecting primitive Christian hymnody), includes the Kyrie. Its return to use in Protestant liturgy links the present with the ancient beginnings of the church, and suggests in these opening moments of worship that the church on earth is linked in praise with the worship of the Church Glorious.

The confession of sin used at this point is a preparation of the people for worship. The psychological objections to the traditional Anglican forms suggested by H. A. Williams, one of the group known as the Cambridge Theologians,[9] is bringing into use the shortened version of the confession from the Roman rite as developed by the Taizé community (Reformed) in France:

We confess to God Almighty, the Father, the Son and the Holy Spirit, before the whole company of the faithful, that we have sinned exceedingly in thought, word, and deed, through our fault, our own fault, our own most grievous fault — wherefore we pray God to have mercy upon us.
Almighty God have mercy upon us, forgive us our sins, and deliver us from evil, confirm and strengthen us in all goodness, and bring us to everlasting life. Amen.[10]

In the Taizé form, the confession is made by the minister to the people, who absolve him, then by the people to the minister, who absolves them. Thus it becomes a practice of mutual confession and assurance of forgiveness.

The reading from the Scriptures follows. Protestant services have sometimes incorporated the Ten Commandments at this point or, in briefer form, the Summary of the Law, as in Luke 10:27. The Roman Mass does not include this. The present trend is toward its omission, perhaps because the epistle reading often incorporates the Christian formulation of law.

The collect for the day is the introduction of the theme. This simple collecting of thoughts into one petition points toward the lesson which the congregation is about to hear. The early liturgies do not suggest that the Old Testament was used in Christian worship (but who were the " prophets " mentioned by Justin?). When included, the Old Testament is a link with the synagogue service and Jewish heritage. The Lutheran liturgy includes three lessons; other liturgies suggest a first lesson from the Prophets or Epistles. The epistle reading recalls the fact that these apostolic letters were used in the earliest assemblies for worship. In the traditional lectionaries the epistles are usually " teaching " passages, prescriptions of how a Christian lives or witnesses to the gospel story. Thus the epistle reading (Romans 12:16-21) for the third Sunday in Epiphany, the season of the " showing forth " of God in Christ, contains the passage: " If your enemy is hungry, feed him. . . . Do not be overcome by evil but overcome evil with good." This is followed by the gospel narratives in Matt. 8:1-13 in which Jesus heals two " enemies " of the people: a leper, despised and set apart from society, and the servant of a centurion, the representative of the feared and hated Roman power.[11] A psalm used responsively or in unison is participation in the heritage of the temple worship and the praise of the people of God across many generations. This closes with the use of the Gloria Patri, a Trinitarian ending to suggest the Christian incorporation in the Psalter. In the Roman rite, this has been shortened to the gradual, selected verses from The Psalms to be used as a hymn between the first and second lessons.

The reading of the gospel is the climax of the service of the Word. Traditionally, all have stood for this reading, respecting the fact that these are the words spoken by the Lord to his people. This is the good news to be heard in solemn gladness. It is introduced by a gradual, a sung response or hymn stanza, and surrounded by the acclamations of the people. " Thanks be to God " and " Praise be to thee, O Christ." Thus are all involved in the preparation for and reception of this Word.

The preaching is meant to be the explication of the Word from Scripture, and this fact is emphasized when preaching follows immediately upon the readings. Here is where the Bible becomes related to the lives of Christians in the world: they hear the Word of God addressed to them as a holy community, called out and sent forth to express their faith in action. The preaching is a serious work in the minister's calling. This role is emphasized personally when he is the reader of the particular passage from which he intends to preach, whether it be Old Testament, Epistle, or Gospel. In reading the gospel, he becomes Christ's representative to the people in the recital of this Word.

In the early centuries, catechumens were dismissed at this point. Their dismissal is still announced in a phrase used in Eastern liturgies: " Let the learners depart; close the doors." They were under instruction, and not yet admitted to the confession of faith or to the prayer of the church.

Having heard the Word read and explained, the people rise to confess their faith in God, although this reaffirmation of the baptismal words is not necessarily a weekly event. Note that it is not meant to express belief *about* but to witness to belief *in* God. The creeds leave broad areas for interpretation. The Anglican and Roman Catholic

Churches use the Nicene Creed, first formulated at the Council of Nicaea in A.D. 325 when the church first became recognized in the Empire, and later revised at the Council of Constantinople in 381. Lutheran and other communions use the Apostles' Creed, or Roman Symbol, half of which predates the Nicene Creed, the third section having been written later. The United Church of Christ offers as a third alternative their recent reformulation of a Statement of Faith. Some persons concerned with liturgical rethinking suggest that the Creed was originally a baptismal formulary in which all joined with the newly baptized in the affirmation of faith, and that it therefore need be used only when Baptism precedes the Eucharistic service. The Roman rite requires it on Sundays and major feasts.

The offertory is a more important part of the service than the worshipers sometimes realize. This is the point at which, having heard and received the Word, they respond in the giving of themselves. There are several parts, and the order is not necessarily fixed. Where there is a choir anthem, it should come at this point, for it is their offering of praise (hopefully the words and music will advance the understanding and action of the service). The gifts of money are collected from the people — this being their offering and action. The offering is brought forward in a procession by lay people (deacons in some traditions, for the gifts represent service) as the people rise to signify their participation in what is happening. Where the service of the Lord's Supper follows, the offerings of bread and wine are also brought in this procession to be received for their intended use. The celebrant, receiving the gifts, offers the prayer of thanksgiving and blessing.

The prayers of petition and intercession made by the people are also a part of the offering to God while they confidently await his acceptance of their needs and his furtherance of their hopes. In Protestant churches generally this is known as the " pastoral prayer," sometimes impromptu, but more usually formulated in advance by the minister.

In Anglican churches this is known, from its introduction, as " the prayer for the whole state of Christ's Church " (" whole " meaning " healthy "). In liturgical rethinking, there are suggestions of how to make this more fully the people's prayer, gathered together by the minister. One form is by the use of collects, each followed by the " Amen " of the people. The litany with its congregational response is another possibility. This is the moment in which the church gathered together in the Spirit asks that God fulfill his promise. So they pray for the world, for the church, and for the specific concerns of the neighborhood, parish, and individual members. Some congregations, seeking to reawaken the sense of community in order to express this personal need in prayer, begin with announcements: a meeting to be held, a marriage to be contracted, a new baby born, a member in the hospital. Then the petitions that follow ask for a blessing on the meeting, pray by name for those to be married, give thanks for the mother's health and the infant's arrival, pray for the recovery of the sick one.

International strife, community problems, parish events, and individual involvements in these happenings are areas of prayer for a congregation of faithful people believing that their Lord knows and cares. The offering of petition closes with the prayer of the church, the Lord's Prayer, which is the summation of the petition of God's faithful people, voicing their assurance that he will fulfill his promises in his own time and according to his good purposes. Whether the Doxology (Matthew) is to be used or omitted (Luke) varies. Whether this offering of prayer should precede or follow the offering of gifts is an open question at present, but experimental liturgies tend to favor the " preceding " position. More important is the realization by the worshiping congregation that this is a part of the liturgy — their common work — part of their offering in faith and love and trust. The offering ends with the sharing of the Peace, " The peace of the Lord be with you," and the re-

ply, " And with you too " (or, " And with your spirit ").
In the Church of South India the greeting by clasped hands
is passed through the congregation and this practice is generally followed among other churches that use the Peace.

The offertory introduces the liturgy of the Lord's Supper. On days when the celebration is not to be completed,
the people sing a hymn and are dismissed with a blessing
which sends them out into everyday life. During the week
they will work, read the Scriptures, and pray separately,
but be conscious of their oneness in Christ.

By whatever name it is called, the Lord's Supper is
meant to be a celebration. It is a joyous event, and this accounts for the present popularity of the term " Eucharist,"
derived from the Greek word meaning " thanksgiving." It
is an act of remembrance, and in Biblical language " remembrance " means " to make present." We do this in
ordinary life. We say, " Do you remember when . . . ? "
and suddenly it seems as if the past event were present in
the moment. We are there. So Christians in the Eucharistic
event are in the upper room, by the Lake of Galilee, with
the multitude being fed, with the couple at Emmaus. That
" there " is here and now. The promise is fulfilled; the
Lord is in the midst of his people, breaking the bread,
offering himself to them. Eastern Christian rites have expressed the awe, the wonder, and the thanksgiving of this
holy Presence much more joyfully than have Western rites,
but the simplicity of Western usage can focus intently on
the action.

The opening is a hymn of praise introduced by the invi-
tional command: " Lift up your hearts," to which the people reply, " We lift them up unto the Lord." The hymn
of praise that follows, " Holy, Holy, Holy, Lord God of
Sabaoth; Heaven and earth are full of thy glory," is reminiscent both of Isaiah's vision in the Temple, and the
praise of the heavenly host in the book of Revelation. The
church temporal joins with the church eternal in joyous
acclaim. The prayer of consecration that follows incorpo-

rates the words of institution. This is the prayer which Justin indicates as unformulated and which took rough form in the second century. To offer it is the responsibility of the presiding minister. It includes the remembrance of God's work for us in Christ's sacrifice, the offering of the lives of the worshipers in thanksgiving for God's gift. If the Lord's Prayer is not used earlier, it belongs here as the Christian community consciously becomes at one with the first disciples. After the Communion of the people comes a brief prayer of thanksgiving and the dismissal.

This is the service which has been at the heart of Christian worship. It is today a Sunday celebration in Catholic, Anglican, and Disciples of Christ congregations, although both the form and meaning vary. But in the amazing openness characterizing the liturgical movement today, the Disciples are rethinking the simplified nineteenth-century American understanding of the origins of the office in order to stress the thanksgiving and to sound the Biblical depths of the word "memorial," while the Roman rite, from a quite different approach, is recovering the fuller participation of the people in the Communion itself. Theological differences remain, but a common sensitivity to the gift is apparent. "Behold, I stand at the door and knock; if anyone hears my voice and opens the door, I will come in to him and eat with him, and he with me" (Rev. 3:20), says the Lord to his people in the church at Laodicea, and they, with all the churches addressed in Revelation, and we in the worldwide church today can say with joy, "Amen. Come, Lord Jesus!" (ch. 22:20). For he comes to each as his people gather together, even as he shall come in glory to be their judge and savior.

IMPLICATIONS FOR EDUCATION

This brief look at the development of the worship of the church and its present forms of becoming suggests several areas of thought with pertinence to education for worship as well as education through worship.

1. Worship is the action of the whole congregation; therefore each person must be taught how to take his part. Only when he understands what he is doing can he fully participate in the action. Otherwise, he is indifferent, confused, or going through words and motions meaninglessly. Many people seemingly prefer an inactive participation. It is easier. Transferral of responsibility from minister to people is not enthusiastically endorsed by all. Many Christians prefer a clergyman-oriented service. It is his work; not theirs. Education for the acceptance of such responsibility must precede education in how to perform this common work.

2. Liturgy as common work requires response from the people. This means a willingness to understand why the congregation sits, stands, and/or kneels as forms of participation. It means that the people take seriously their role vis-à-vis the minister, whether it be in mutual blessing, mutual assurance, in the assenting " Amens," responsive verses, psalms and other hymns. None of this can be taken for granted. The use of hymnals (how numerous they are!) is traditional in Protestant denominations, but the singing is often indifferent. The reading from The Psalms has been cut to a minimum and sometimes omitted (and the " readings " are too often other Biblical passages never intended for responsive or unison use). " Amens " in recent years have belonged to the Anglicans and the sect groups.

3. Congregational worship includes specific roles for particular individuals: choir members, readers of the lessons, perhaps acolytes, deacons, or others to collect and bring forward all the offerings. The readers are the " new " factor. It is a serious responsibility to read the Word of God in Scripture for the edification (upbuilding) of a congregation. This requires thoughtful reading, prayer, and practice. It is a form of mutual service.

4. The offertory in its wholeness needs to be taken more

seriously. It is not a mundane matter to be hidden under the sound of music, with the results whisked discreetly out of sight at the earliest moment. The money literally represents the life of the people, for time is life, and life is work, and work earns money. This is one facet of offering our lives to God. The bringing up of the materials for the Communion is a reminder that in earlier days people brought loaves of bread which they had baked, and at one point in history, as Justin describes it, the eucharistized bread was taken after the service to those unable to be present. The anthem is the offering of the gifts of the singers; it is not the whole offering, but it is indeed part. So too are the prayers and petitions of the people offered for God's use and blessing. Hence it is important to consider including with these prayers the litany response or the " Amens " to a series of collects.

5. The liturgy needs to be an action — full but simple, beautiful and meaningful, filled with joy and thanksgiving. It has both form (structure) and rhythm (movement). In the service of the Word the people hear God address them in Scripture and sermon; in the offertory they respond to him in gifts and prayer; in the Eucharist, God and man meet in a mutual action of consecration — the breaking of the bread, Communion and thanksgiving: Emmanuel, that is, " God with us."

6. The note of joy and thanksgiving needs to be strong and vital. It is surprising how one can enter upon a service of Sunday worship and leave with a feeling almost of oppression. The hymns have been sad and sentimental, the Scripture reading has been brief and didactic, the sermon has been more of the same, the prayers have been speaking through God to the congregation (or telling God what he already surely knows) , the offertory anthem has been weak. What happened? The service was concentrated on the congregation as a collection of individuals — their personal thoughts and feelings — with an attempt to speak directly

to their need for assurance or uplift. Whatever place and need there may be for this in Christian worship, it is not in the Sunday gathering.

The classical liturgy now being recovered is addressed to God. The individual's uplift comes because he is freed from himself, enabled to respond to One who is among and yet beyond. In praise and thanksgiving, in a true Biblical remembrance and re-presentation, the worshiper becomes more fully himself, more surely alive, more enabled to face the hard realities of existence. Christ lives and dies again for each of us because he did this for all. To see just the first part is not only self-centered but even uncertain. How can one know only from personal experience? Because he saved Peter and Mary, Paul and Justin, and has offered his salvation to all others, so we may with more assurance assert that this is for us — for me, for you, for all. This is what is meant by objectivity in worship, and this alone keeps the church away from romanticism and unreality and sets its purpose in clear focus. The work of the Christian church is made known as the church listens to what God has to say — and this is not necessarily for its comfort, but always for its strengthening.

There are or should be other forms of worship: for evenings, for the opening of study sessions, for retreats, for families, for personal devotion. Here is a wide-open area for development, and how little creativity has been shown in the development of such occasions for worship! This account is intended simply to elucidate and explain the primary form of the church's worship, indicating present developments and variations. The structure is given. But each young Christian and each newly baptized Christian needs to be taught by others the words, the actions, the meanings of the service and how to participate in it, so that he may recognize that his presence is necessary and that his participation is an act of loving and faithful obedience to God his Savior.

CHAPTER 2

THE PERSON
WHO WORSHIPS

A N EXPLORATION OF THE HISTORY and development of
worship brings a chronological dimension into understanding, but there are other factors. The person brings
himself to worship and participates in common with all
who surround him. The understanding of the worshiping
self is a part of the understanding of worship.

UNDERSTANDING GOD

Worship begins with an attitude, for one must decide
to attend the service. The reasons are not always so simple
as they appear on the surface to be. Worship is a habit. The
inner core of a congregation is made up of those who attend faithfully week after week. Scarcely anyone feels like
doing this every time the day rolls around. (There are
even times when one does not want to eat.) While such a
habit could be compulsive and based on guilt (" I'd feel
uncomfortable if I didn't go "), it can also be based, positively, on an objective sense of responsibility. It affirms that
participation in worship is primarily for the purpose of
praising God rather than of being personally inspired. It
sees that the presence of each member is necessary for the
fullest expression of the worship of the congregation.

Worship implies belief in One who is beyond the self. There are several attitudes held, ranging from atheism (where one is unable to accept either the existence of or the relationship to the supernatural) through agnosticism ("It might be so, or then again it might not"), to doubt ("Yes, but maybe —") into faith ("I believe"). Faith is not belief *about* but belief *in,* as commentators on the creedal formulas have reminded us. Intrinsic to this kind of belief is relationship, which means the ability of the worshiper to relate, in this case, to One who is unseen and yet accepted as real. The elements of trust and of surrender enter here. It is also possible for the worshiper to look on his participation in worship from an intellectual level, or as politely following custom, or as continuing in a familiar pattern. These are ways of "standing off" relationships and avoiding the necessity of giving and responding. The inner dynamics of personality enter into the way in which individuals participate in worship. Moreover, since corporate worship is involved here, the ability to relate to other people is another factor. The proximity of others should encourage and deepen participation, but this happens only where there is openness to receive. Some people try to sit in a corner where they will be alone; others say they do not come to church because they can worship better by themselves. This is an oversimplification, a quick answer which not only avoids relationship within the community but also avoids facing seriously the many reasons that can impede such participation. These reasons cannot be forced into the open; they can only emerge gradually as a person is willing and enabled to move toward involvement with other human beings.

Negatively, belief can involve fear. "I am not sure what God is like, but it is best to do what I think I ought to" or, "God will punish me if I do not go to church." Not all compulsive action is given this sort of overt explanation; the act may simply follow an irrational sense of "ought."

Going more deeply, one might ask: " If you are not sure, why do you assume you must? " or, " Why do you think guilt and punishment are involved in not attending church? " Anything known about God has developed from individual experiences, the shared experiences of fellow Christians, the internalizing of what has been read or told by others from the Bible, and the historic experience of the Christian community.

Positively, belief promises fulfillment (but not perfection). The awareness of God and the closeness to others who are similarly devoted to him adds another dimension to living and to the whole area of relationships. This answers the aspirations of people toward a fulfillment they cannot completely explain. It assures them of acceptance by One who understands, an acceptance that they can only fully know if the community also accepts them and thereby helps them toward self-adequacy and self-acceptance. The proclamation of the good news is that we are made just by him; and this is an assurance which all but the most self-righteous need to hear repeated.

Worship is part of the integration of the self around God. " We can only worship in the measure and the form that our development permits," says Roy S. Lee.[12] This development begins at birth, for the self which has found relationship in the nourishing mother and the protecting father is the self which can believe that these terms apply to God. The infant learns to trust because someone warm and loving is always near to answer his cry and fulfill his needs. Deep within the recesses of his being, he will always carry the memory of those first two years. If he is deprived at this time, he can indeed learn later to trust other people (and trust himself to them) and God, but there will always be a reserve, so that some act of will is needed to make this attitude of trust possible. During the next two years the child is learning to accept the cultural demands of society, to give up his will when necessary, and to accept as his own

the will of others for him. " No," says the two-year-old with
great emphasis. If his resistance is met with anger and
punishment, he will hold deep within himself a sense of
shame and guilt, finding it difficult to expose himself and
to be outgoing lest someone, figuratively at least, slap him.
Being " sensitive," he will always try to protect with pride
a too tender ego. Such a person may indeed learn through
later experience to make friends and to be generous toward
others, but he will find it difficult to make the complete
and open surrender of himself which alone can yield the
fullest communion with man and with God. Note that this
yielding is not submission, which is a forced attitude growing out of guilt and covering anger; surrender is freely
given and assumes joyous acceptance. This has always been
the aim of the religious life and the basis for the joy received through worship.[13]

The Christian language often uses the term " Father "
with reference to God. This comes inevitably from the
address in the Lord's Prayer, the " Our Father." It reflects
the fact that Jesus in several places in the New Testament
addressed God as Father, and when speaking to the disciples, referred to him as " your heavenly Father." It follows that the meaning of the word in its human reference
will color the meaning of the word in its divine reference.
Nobody who lives in a world of reality thinks of parents as
perfect — either his own or himself as a parent. But this
knowledge can be hidden deep inside the self, especially if
one has connected love and acceptance with perfection.
Since God, by classical definition, is perfect (whatever that
may mean to the definer), similar questions about accept-
ability and worthiness to be loved may enter into the feelings of the believer.

The small child, around the age of four or five, begins
to see his mother and father in a new light. Of course the
little boy loves his mother, who has supplied his every
need, so now he says, " I'm going to marry Mommy when

I grow up." Really, he knows that he cannot do this, for his father has already married her. Is he jealous? He and his father are so much alike that he begins to identify with his father. He is already a little man, and his father becomes the strong, courageous figure with whom he identifies. So, too, God is always to him, in some way, the powerful One. If the little boy finds himself unable to identify with his father, but only fears him, then God can only mean fear to him, and true relationship can hardly develop.

Likewise, the little girl loves her mother, the source of all comfort, but she smiles and says, " I'm Daddy's girl." She knows, of course, that Mother belongs to Daddy, and she senses her likeness to her mother. Eventually this becomes in her the promise of being a mother who nurtures babies. This little girl is on the way to becoming a little mother. Fathers protect mothers and babies and little girls; a father is one in whom is found security and peace. So this warmth and trust can become a part of a woman's response to God, unless she also has found that her father does not protect and does not give security.

Horace Mann, the nineteenth-century educator who was a founder of the American public-school system, tells with regret that he was never able to feel the presence of God as he knew some other people did. He grew up in a sternly " puritan " family in which the terror of the wrath and judgment of God hung over his head. As an adult, he became, with many of his generation, Unitarian, for that fellowship challenged the rigid interpretation of the Christian faith, and emphasized the humanness of God in Jesus. It was too late for God to be to Horace Mann anything but a Being who existed, in whom he believed intellectually but to whom he could not relate.

This story suggests some elements in the response to God within the worship of a congregation. Each person brings his own understanding, which comes out of his own background and development. Because of this fact, some of the materials of worship will have references which may cause avoidance reactions in some participants. Such a factor needs to be kept in mind by those who choose materials. Some people may be helped by examining the roots of their reactions. A different approach may be useful with, for example, those persons who link certain hymns pleasurably with their childhood and wish to sing them for that reason alone.

RELATIONSHIP TO GOD

The Old Testament frequently described the relationship between God and his people through the imagery of marriage. They were covenanted to each other for life. God sustained his people and they supposedly turned their lives toward him in obedience and service. Frequently his people were unfaithful and disobedient, wandering off to serve other gods. So in the New Testament, marriage is likened to the relationship between Christ and the church, his people. He loves them and gives himself for them; they surrender to him. This reciprocal relationship depicts the dynamic quality of revelation and response in worship.

One concrete expression of this relationship is through prayer. In words, thoughts, feelings, the believer expresses his love and trust or his guilt and anxiety. Sometimes he longs for and clings to this avenue of expression; at other times he avoids it or uses it indifferently. It cannot be assumed that because someone " got nothing from the service " that there was some great lack in the form or content of it. Perhaps other persons both gave and received in worship. How an individual reacts to the words of prayer within the service depends on the expression of them and on the interpretation of the worshiper (see Chapter 4 on prayer) . Prayer can condemn; it can also bring the words of assurance. Some people cannot believe this, even when they hear it said. This is not true to their experience. For others, prayer can be the affirmation of acceptance, the source of assurance through which aspiration is encouraged, and the reality of God's love affirmed.

This depends partly on how the conscience has been developed, sometimes described as the " internalized parent." When the child is five or six years old, he learns to hear the parent's voice inside. If the parent has been used to issuing orders all the time, the child will be constantly alert to obey this inner voice. If the parent has given him some freedom to make decisions, the child will feel free to make his own best decision when an either/or arises. He begins to develop responsibility and to act on his own initiative without a feeling of guilt, without saying, " How would Dad act? " or, " What would Mother want me to do? "

Some people use religion (and are encouraged to do so) to reinforce this conscience or superego. Now God the Father becomes the authority who gives the rules, lays down the law. How much more effective than the human parent, for the child is taught that God is everywhere, knows everything! Now if he disobeys, he has disobeyed God. If God is more feared than loved, the resultant effect on the relationship to God is understandable. The law of the parent has become the law of God. Church schools can unwittingly reinforce this idea. A teacher was telling a class of third-grade children a story about a bear who disobeyed his mother and nearly got left out in the cold. Then she said, " Draw a picture of a law we are supposed to obey, any law — God's law or Mother's law." The casual tone of " any law " conveyed, whether the teacher realized this or not, that the two were roughly equivalent. It would have been interesting to talk more with the boy who disregarded the teacher's suggestion and instead drew a picture of a child writing on the blackboard: "$4 + 3 = 7$." Here was law beyond the reach of conscience!

Some people project this perfect law on God in a way to sanctify their conduct. They grow to believe that whatever seems right and righteous to them, must have been ordained by God. They can educe Biblical, theological, or ecclesiastical reasons to back them up. This has led to religious tyranny in which people have fought to bring others to their way of life by " proving " it to be the divine will.

If a person feels that he must keep the law perfectly in order to merit the love of God, he must do something to convince himself that he is doing so, for he needs this love. No one is perfect. What can happen? Such a person becomes blind to his own wrongdoing. He assures people that he is doing all things for their good, or that this must be right because it is God's will. He covers his own uneasiness with pride. Then he transfers the sense of sin to others. He is always judging them, disparaging them: " This is good, but . . ."; " He means well, but . . ."; " If only he had done it so . . ." By tearing down others, he is able to build up himself. By seeing the imperfection of others, he is able to believe that he is better than they are. This is what happened to the Pharisees in the New Testament. They were very good people, eager to keep the Law so that God might dwell among his people, but they ended up by overreaching, by excluding others because they made it so difficult even for themselves. It happened among the Puritans, who so limited the qualifications for the elect that most of the people of the community could not qualify for membership in the church. It is a sincerely held doctrine of some Christian groups today. Their worship has a certain purity to them because it is entered into only by those who hold a certain standard of living. The pitfalls in such an interpretation of conscience and worship are serious. Realistically oriented people know that perfection is an unattainable ideal. Commentaries exegeting Matt. 5:48 usually agree that " be perfect " must be interpreted in the light of the Greek root, which in the New Testament means " fulfillment " or " goal," and which usually refers to God's fulfillment in his Kingdom, the Parousia. Fulfillment and perfection are not necessarily the same. To be fulfilled is to be fully human, but to be fully human is not to become God. This is the mistake the perfectionists make.

When perfectionism becomes a strong note in the service of worship, some people will avoid the congregation because they feel uncomfortable, and, sensing that their fellows are living under illusion, react against such unreality. Those who have some personal necessity for holding this point of view (security, or, " A person should be good, and I am good ") under the impulse of reality soon become judgmental toward others, including the minister. Such congregations can have a long history of friction and even of division. Some become unable to face themselves and to rejoice in being human because this involves being sinful. Trying to become perfect, they live under guilt and tension.

Symbols and Worship

Symbols are a way of interpreting meaning that involves the whole person. Words can define, but definition sets a boundary. A symbol is open-ended and has many meanings. Symbols are often pictorial (iconic), but gestures and other actions are also symbolic. Dress is symbolic; figures of speech in the Bible or in hymnody are symbolic; even the arrangement of a church and the furnishings hold connotative meaning. The study of a symbol clarifies its many-sidedness. Meaning is more realized than explained. Symbols can convey emotion, and so be reminders that worship is not only intellectual but involves the whole self. Personal meanings enter into symbols. Contemplation of a symbol releases the ability to respond.

Symbols have historically acquired associations, but they

also take on the interpretations projected by the viewers. There is no way of preventing this, and it points both to the added resources of this personal dimension and the need to realize that it always comes into play. The response to a symbol is often positive, but negative feelings may also be included. Sometimes the intellectual description of a symbol is quite different from an emotional description that a person could give. Guilt, expiation, sensuality — all surround the symbol and may persuade a person to withdraw in discomfort. To see why the symbol becomes invested with added meanings is to gain understanding of the religious expression of the self. Unconscious factors enter into thinking, however much one tries to repress them. More likely, they then simply become displaced and are less easily handled. As Roy S. Lee points out, " Where unconscious notions are hidden, there is rationalizing instead of reasoning." [14]

For example, the cross is the central symbol of the Christian faith. What does it mean? Some speakers point to a neon-lighted cross and cry out lustily, " We are saved by the blood of the cross." There is triumph, satisfaction, and enjoyment in the tone. Other people, hearing this, may withdraw in extreme discomfort. Blood to them is frightening. It means pain, torture, death. Others have an uncertain feeling of guilt; why should one be saved by someone else's blood? Fear, guilt, discomfort — all of these hide a smoldering anger, for anger is the body's defense against attack, and those who are angry have heard the speaker's word as an attack. " Christ died for you; what are you doing for him? " one is asked. Some turn aside, saying deep within, " No one died for me; I take care of myself." Others set about doing good works; they didn't ask for this, but they will try to make it up anyway. To know that good works can be a way of overcoming guilt is not to disparage them but only to understand one wellspring of human activity.

Many people have come to terms with pain, blood, and death. They have accepted the fact that our lives depend on other lives and the correlative that other human beings need us. They have learned how to give and to receive, and in varying ways they have explored the meanings of love, knowing that it is both demanding and rewarding, joyous and painful, requited and rebuffed. Anything that is said by intellectual explanation about the cross is filled in by each individual according to the deeper dimensions of his understanding about life. Only when an understanding in some way touches this dimension can it begin to act on the personal interpretations in such a way as to make them positive and strengthening. The Biblical use of the symbol can be helpful, for beginning with the reality of a historical situation, accepted in its many implications, the interpretations help the believer to identify with the Crucified One as a path into newness of life in which the whole self seems changed. Some hymns can do this when they are faithful to Biblical interpretations. Others become merely startling or sentimental.

When people have the opportunity of expressing feelings, they become better able to understand them, to reflect upon them, and to develop the possibility of insight and a new kind of response. When worship is oriented toward God, one of the benefits is a growing and persisting healing of the brokenness in all persons, a bent toward wholeness. It is good to be reminded that the root meaning of salvation is " healing."

As law comes from the superego, conscience (whether as overwhelming demand or as the security of boundaries), love comes from the id, the libido. This is the free-flowing, energizing warmth of which the Bible says we are capable because God has first loved us. The acceptance of love and learning how to channel it creatively make possible the fullest human living. This assumes an ability both to give and to receive. Sometimes this possibility arouses only fear, a withdrawal of the self. When a person is able freely and openly to reflect within himself upon a symbol, the barriers of fear can be broken and love released. Since such love is powerful, many human beings, including some religious people, are afraid of this power. If a rigid conscience holds back the free-flowing response to a symbol, the rich possibilities of worship are diminished. Often the repression breaks through and becomes sentimentality. In Catholicism this takes the form of visual symbols — a bleeding heart, for instance; in Protestantism it is most often found in hymns such as " In the Garden " (" He walks with me and he talks with me, and he tells me I am his own "), with an accompanying sentimental melody. The person with a sure sense of himself, of ego-identity, can accept the warm power of the id and be free to serve a reality-oriented superego rather than a sentimental, idealistic, or perfectionist conscience.

As symbols that are seen or read have diverse power according to the personal interpretation, so also have the symbols that are enacted. Action involves the whole person, and there is need within a service for rhythm and motion, a change of mood and of pace. Physical posture both expresses attitude and predisposes toward one, but no one posture necessarily encourages a specific attitude. Congregations usually stand to sing, and this encourages an outgoing response, but a meditative hymn is sometimes sung seated. In American churches one usually sits or kneels to pray, but in the German Lutheran tradition one stands. Most congregations are used to being seated to hear the Scriptures read, but in several traditions the people rise for the reading of the gospel lesson. A set of meanings cluster around each action and affect the total response of the person participating in congregational worship. Similarly for the Lord's Supper, some congregations express the sense of unified fellowship as they remain seated and are served; others go forward to surround the table, standing or kneeling, each form in its own way expressing the corporate meaning of this act of thanksgiving.

The arrangement of the services expresses meaning in its progression. In the recent generations of American Protestantism, this has sometimes been lost sight of when ministers or congregations were individually the arbiters of how a service should be planned. Such freedom could be creative, but it can also lead to variety without unity, originality without cohesion, and an emphasis on individual preferences. It will not be easy for local congregations to surrender this right and accept a general pattern with allowable variations as planned by a wider church body. Such a service, as evidenced in several liturgies recently proposed, moves from praise outthrust toward God (call to worship, invocation, hymn) to the hearing and learning of God's word to his people (lessons, psalms, sermon), followed by their response in offering to him (affirmation of faith, intercessions, collection of money and of the elements for the Lord's Supper when that is celebrated), and the sending forth into the world (hymns of praise, blessing).

THE LORD'S SUPPER

The Lord's Supper stems from the historical action of Jesus in sharing a meal with his disciples on the night in which he was betrayed, and Christian rites have always incorporated the retelling of that event, usually in the tradition that the apostle Paul said was handed on to him as recorded in I Cor., ch. 11. It is frequently spoken of as a celebration, suggesting a joyous quality. This puts a different focus on the Supper from what has sometimes been evident in Western rites, where there has been a strong emphasis on the sacrificial, forgetting that the service can be joyous, and in general expressing a polemical theology of the atonement. There is reason to believe that this should be the joyous recollection of a meal shared in the presence of the Lord, the evidence of his presence among his people, and the promise of his final triumphant return. Here is a symbolic action through which love and warmth should be expressed among a closely knit fellowship. Too often, however, it arouses uncomfortable feelings, guilt, and thinly veiled antipathy. Even the words of institution: " This is my body . . ."; " This cup is the new covenant in my blood . . ." evoke responses similar to feelings aroused by references to the cross, no matter how the words are rationalized, intellectualized, symbolized, demythologized, or otherwised explained.

Now it could be helpful, if one were of so open a mind, to face the possibility that this rite has a long history, going back into prehistoric centuries long before the Christian era. The eating and drinking of the person, whether actually or symbolically, was not only a way of transferring the great worth of the person to others, but was a deep and literal bond among the members. We have no way of entering into the emotional patterns of aboriginal man, but there is no need to look down on him because our needs are expressed so differently. Even the Old Testament suggests that the firstborn among some peoples was sacrificed as a gift of thanksgiving for fertility. The people of Israel were bidden to substitute one of the flock. Substitutionary sacrifice of thanksgiving was being offered for the gift of love.

Once, on a particular day, the body of Jesus was indeed offered up in death, and this event has always surrounded the celebration of the Lord's Supper. The event deepens the awesomeness of his last hours among his disciples, the mutual love and support shared. The memory has never left his people, but along with it are added the remembrances of other meals shared in the presence of the risen Lord. The Lord's Supper is not the celebration of death but of life. Surrounding this meal, and deriving from its symbolism, should be all the feelings of warmth, fellowship, love, acceptance, and reconciliation. Every important event in life is shared in a meal: the birth of a child, the marriage of young people, the burial of the dead, welcoming the returned, admitting the newcomer, sealing a business activity. It is only natural that a symbolic meal should be at the heart of the rite by which the Christian community worships God.

The order of service provides that the bread and wine be brought forward as a part of the offertory. This reflects an early custom when families supplied the materials needed for the Supper. Today this is done to emphasize the ordinary, everyday quality of these materials through which is expressed the communion between God and his people. It further symbolizes the offering of Christ, who according to the words of the apostle, " loved us and gave himself for us." Pressing further, it must be said that included here is the offering of the worshiper, indeed of the whole congregation: the surrender of the self in joyous abandon before the love of God. " We offer unto thee ourselves, our souls and bodies," as one form puts it. The individual, trusting and open, receives his Lord and gladly goes forth to obedient service. The congregation, one body around the Holy Table, expresses the mutuality of the love that exists among Christians because it is sent from God. How appropriate are two symbolic gestures: the Peace, in which a handclasp is passed from person to person among the congregation, and the closing words, in which the people are sent into their daily life.

Worship gives release to the pent-up feelings that people bring to the gathering of Christians. Through all the elements of the service, the order, the motions, the symbols of varied forms, people find wholeness and renewed strength. Here they are free to give and to receive. They can be released from egocentricity, and be enabled to turn outward to serve the needs of the world. Not all do this, of course. Many feed their anxieties, cover up their disparagement of service, minister, and congregation, and use the service for self-oriented needs. But it need not be so if there is the slightest openness to explore the self, believing that the grace of God sustains and heals. One can neither ignore the self nor dwell on the self unduly, but rather make a deliberate effort to turn the self toward God, who will show one the brother man.

RELIGIOUS BELONGING

Participation in congregational worship hinges in large part on a sense of religious belonging. Where the geographical parish still exists, as it does in the suburbs, the prevailing real estate practice of grouping houses according to price ensures that each congregation will be composed largely of specific socioeconomic groups. Where people tend to choose the church to which they belong, or at least the church which they attend, as in cities, they choose according to needs for formality or informality, a high level of performance by minister and/or choir, or the active involvement of the congregation, intellectuality or simplicity, openness of ideas or firmness of convictions. Even Roman Catholics, although technically attached to a parish, have been known to gravitate on Sunday to the place where the interpretation of the liturgy " speaks " to them whether by way of familiarity or of newness. Enough studies have been made of the development of religious groups from " sect " to " church " type to indicate that the person who feels most excluded from the civic community finds his needed sense of acceptance in the religious community. The fact of social participation as a factor in religious belonging cannot be evaded. Here a person has a sense of identification; his worth as a person is recognized. This security makes him feel " at home," and with anxiety thus lessened he is able to relax and enjoy the service. If churches are indeed filled with like-minded people, there are good psychological reasons for this fact.

The Canadian sociologist of religion Hervé Carrier uses the term "attitude" to denote a basic factor in religious belonging.[15] This is the disposition which a person holds toward a group that influences how he shall act with reference toward it. Both the person and the environment are involved. The sense of belonging *is* the attitude of a person within his church group.

> His belonging is no longer a fact viewed from the exterior, a fact reported to a census-taker, or a religious category; it is a psychosocial reality. The member sees himself as taking part in his group; he identifies himself with it, he participates in it, he receives his motivation from it; in a word, he is in a state or disposition of interaction with the group, which understands, inspires and welcomes him. He belongs to his group and the "psychological structure of his disposition with regard to the group" constitutes his specific attitude of belonging.[16]

The individual has a sense of identification within this worshiping community, he feels himself to be a participant in its action and life, and it in turn motivates his attitudes and responses in other areas of life.

Such a group has cohesion, for it is made up of people who are interdependent. Cohesion is not found in a group made up of people who come together simply for individual goal needs, as for example those who attend a three-day conference or an evening workshop — hence the pathos in the leave-taking of the young people at a summer conference who promise faithfully to get together for the Christmas-week reunion. Nor is cohesion found in a group made up largely of dependent people, each of whom has come primarily to have individual needs met. The cohesive group is formed by those who need both to give and to receive support; the emphasis is on mutuality. It is not independence or dependence, but interdependence. Such a group has strong roots.

This kind of security makes possible cooperation, another characteristic of the cohesive group. If a person is not threatened, he is able to help others, even to give up private viewpoints and goals in working toward the good of the whole. The cohesive group holds goals in common, and individual members are able to accept the discipline of loyalty and obedience to these goals.

To be sure there are varied reasons why a person, once in a group, remains there. In a positive way, the group attracts and holds the loyalty of its members. " We want you," they seem to say, and the person responds. Sometimes, in the depth of his being, there is secret fear of being excluded. " Suppose they do not want me? " he says to himself, and tries to conform to the patterns of the group. Groups with a strong sense of the sacramental in their worship or a strong sense of community in social relationships attract by positive motives. Groups with rigid requirements of intellectual belief or a rigid behavior pattern tend to have a negative cohesiveness. Added to this is the strong factor of social prestige which accrues to the " church " type of religious community, and the feeling of social exclusion which is part of the attraction to the " sect " group. This cannot be pressed too far; the Roman Catholic Church was for years the familiar refuge for immigrants living a ghetto existence in American cities; alternatively, some people belong to sect groups from religious convictions regarding their authenticity as Christian communities. Once within a group, a person tends to remain there because of the security it offers in familiarity, the sense of acceptance, the confirmation of his own beliefs and practices. He leaves when any of these is drastically threatened, seeking another group or excluding himself completely from the religious congregation. The external reasons given, however, rarely probe the depths of meaning involved in the break. " The people are cold "; " I don't like the minister's sermons "; " The service is routine "; " They don't live as Christians "; or, "They are tearing down my beliefs " are only part of the reasons why a person absents himself from the worshiping congregation. An awareness of the intricate factors involved in religious belonging guard one against too easily asserting that theological, liturgical, or sociological factors alone will solve such situations.

The cohesion, or at least the attendance, in a worshiping community is strongest where it can be assumed that here lies the means for salvation, that here alone lies a unique part of the religious life. If attendance is in any way " necessary," the group meeting week after week becomes strongly knit. In the community where the congregational worship is an optional avenue for religious living, attendance may or may not be large, for the cohesion lies only in the accumulation of the felt needs of each individual. With some groups this produces faithful attendance, each deeming his presence necessary for group maintenance; in others, nonattendance may even become a mark of religious independence. Again, a religious group that is the center of a person's friendships evokes strong loyalty and faithful attendance. His life is centered there, and he is happy in this weekly reunion.

A recent study of religious belonging used several general groupings to indicate degree of involvement: participation in the church as a social group; acceptance of mutually held ethical principles; the sharing of common beliefs. Levels of participation include the completely involved, those who attend faithfully and take roles of lay leadership; those who attend frequently and probably contribute financially; those who attend on special occasions such as Easter. These are the active, regular, marginal, and dormant (nonattending) members.

While more empirical study needs to be done in the area, it seems that the cultural community is a factor in religious belonging. Each congregation within a community is distinctive, colored by the educational level, the economic condition, the social class, and the cultural interests of the majority of its people. This cuts across denominational lines, for in one part of the country a Presbyterian church will be the ranking " first " church, whereas someplace else it might be Baptist, United Church of Christ, Episcopal, or Lutheran. Historical situations enter into this, for the descendants of first settlers tend to become the reigning families of a community. Where there is more than one church of a particular denomination, there will be distinctive differences in the pattern of belonging, especially if the " second " church is in a less economically favored part of town. It will then emphasize smallness, simplicity, and the binding factors of familiarity and spontaneity. Roman Catholic parishes have in the past served ethnic groups, but as has happened with Lutherans and increasingly with the Orthodox, these parishes are now more reflective of the socioeconomic situation of the neighborhood in which the new parish is located.

People are able to identify with a situation that assures them that their cultural needs are " right "; the music might be that of gospel hymns, of nineteenth-century tunes, of seventeenth-century chorales or plainsong; the preaching could be intellectual or emotional, personal or social; the prayers could be prepared or spontaneous; involvement of the congregation could be vocal or aural. These options are expressions of basic worship traditions modified in the direction of cultural needs. The worshiper feels social approval in belonging to one group rather than another, in performing actions in one way rather than another. This may even be a revolt against the forms of childhood, and/or an attempt to express new modes of religious thinking and feeling growing out of changed patterns of life. Unconscious needs are projected into the forms and materials of the service, and the person feels comfortable. Something of this is involved in the saying that one " feels good " after a service or found it " satisfying," " inspiring," or " strengthening." These are some subjective aspects of congregational worship.

Although the first identification with the worshiping community comes through a sense of " belonging," religious maturing involves a process by which the individual thinks through his understanding of faith and practice so that another dimension is added. Now he understands in some measure why he believes and belongs. Some intellectualizing may be a rationale for what one already accepts. There is neither contradiction nor progression between and within the two modes. Both are a necessary part of religious development. There is a belonging which accepts participation with the whole self, enjoying both the mind's understanding of the liturgy and the emotional involvement in its unfolding. Sensitivity to the surrounding members of the congregation who join in praise and petition deepens the action.

The religious community is strengthened through the kind of leadership exercised by the minister,[17] the size of the group (too small a group tends to break into cliques), and the willingness to reach out to others and admit them into the group, which thus is continually being renewed.

IMPLICATIONS FOR EDUCATION

The family is the only other group that the individual enters earlier than the church. Consequently, the original sense of belonging comes before one is conscious of it. The family goes to church; the child goes. First he identifies with his parents' religion, then he identifies with the religious group itself. By the age of twelve he is developing religious convictions of his own and is beginning to participate in worship because of the meanings it holds for him. Even the deliberate abstention from religious involvement which often occurs sometime during adolescence is a part of development. He is assuring himself that he attends worship not because he feels part of his family or of the familiar company which is his church, but rather because of personal decision and commitment.

Education for religious belonging begins when the small child is helped to feel that this is for him. He needs to hear how his parents brought him to the church as an infant and how he was received there before the congregation or its representatives by baptism or dedication. He needs a place where people his own age come together and someone older cares about them. He needs to feel that he is a welcome participant with other adults in the worship of the congregation and that means are taken to help him understand what is happening.

The adolescent, enmeshed in the task of self-identity, has other needs for the religious community. It assures him of continuity with the past, and symbolizes the continuing tie with his family. It assures him that God exists and that he so believes, expressed in the familiar continuities of the order of morning worship. But there are questions. His horizons are expanding in all directions. Is the family to be the authority for church participation? Does this familiar form of worship express what his growing self believes about God? In young adulthood, whether he goes away to college or to work, he will probably try out different churches or no church. The religious preferences of the marriage partner will enter into the later decision. Cultural factors will begin to operate.

A parish will find it helpful to look steadily at the factors that operate within its particular worshiping congregation. It could then see more clearly whether it is really meeting the religious expressions of the people who attend (and perhaps more importantly, those who theoretically could attend but do not). It should recognize the relationship between the hymns (words and music) and the culture; ask if the use of the Scriptures is confined to the familiar or if it covers a broad range of Biblical material; look at the sermon subjects and how these are developed; reflect on the types and uses of prayers; recognize that the programming of the service and its conduct are modifications of a particular tradition to fit cultural patterns. It is a curious fact that some people from deliberately non-liturgical churches seem to take deep satisfaction from an elaborate liturgy, dress, and hierarchical arrangement within fraternal orders.

The educational task lies in the expression of love toward one another within the community wherein each accepts the other, helps the other, and refrains from judgment. This is the basis for positive identification without fear. It suggests a congregational participation in the service that will express and reinforce religious understandings. There needs to be encouragement to accept the new, whether this be new members, new forms in worship, or new avenues for expression in daily life, but such encouragement can only be based on acceptance of the present situation.

In educating for worship, one must remember that the individual brings his own psychological patterns of religion to the group. Worship is indeed a habit, but education seeks to make habits an expression of freedom rather than a pattern of compulsion.

The person's beliefs, shared with the rest of the Christian community, are the basis for his worship; therefore, education needs to help people clarify how belief about God is involved in the relationship to him, expressed in prayer and in other elements of worship.

Since worship involves a number of people, it follows that only those who can relate in some way to other people will be able to share in this act. How can a person be brought out of withdrawal? Worship can do this more effectively than fellowship groups because during worship the person is able to proceed at his own pace. He may simply sit among the congregation, or in a corner, or in the back, sensing the existence of others but going no farther. Yet by standing and sitting, by speaking aloud and listening (all directed toward God), he becomes a participant. The hymns speak of "we"; the prayer begins "Our Father." The minister's words, "The Lord be with you," evoke unhesitating response, "And with you too." The person passes the offering plate, picks up a hymnal, moves toward the door. No one is alone who can bring himself so far as to attend worship; yet such a person holds the initiative as to the mode of his own participation within the congregation.

Educationally, one is conscious of the phases of religious development through which the child has passed and which he brings to his adult understanding of the service of worship. The way in which the worshiper interprets Scripture, hymns, and the address to God in prayer will reflect this fact. Negatively, this means that some will ignore what is heard or will reinterpret or feel uncomfortable. Positively, it means reinforcement through avenues of already internalized religious understandings and feelings. It is made explicit in the way through which these materials explain the character of God and the meaning of the Christian life. There is a world of difference between the didactic "Come, labor on. Who dares stand idle on the harvest plain . . ..?" and the prayerful "O Master, let me walk with Thee in lowly paths of service free."

People need the opportunity, outside the worship service, to react to the forms and materials through study groups or an afterchurch coffee hour. They need to feel the way in which the order of service is developed, to indicate how they understand the song and Scripture, how the sermon speaks, how they feel as they put their money in the offering plates (money has important symbolic significance to everyone), what they think is happening during congregational prayer. Uncomfortable questions with the possibility of uncomfortable reactions? The whole self attends church on Sunday morning. An understanding of the psychological factors and the sociological factors helps in understanding the structure of worship and gives a basis for evaluating both the old forms and the new.

CHAPTER 3 | # THE CONTENT OF WORSHIP

T HE PRIMARY MATERIALS OF WORSHIP are the Scriptures read and preached, the prayers, the singing, and the Lord's Supper. Each has developed its own tradition and each is at a transitional point today.

THE BIBLE

It is generally assumed that the Bible was read in the earliest gatherings for Christian worship. The synagogue had been the place in which the Law and the Prophets were read, and the Jerusalem community participated in its worship. Whether Christian communities, particularly in Gentile lands, also used these Scriptures has been questioned. References in the epistles suggest that the traditions and sayings of Jesus were read and that the writings of the apostles — letters to churches — were read and shared with others. Out of this has grown the custom of having epistle and gospel readings in the rites of Orthodox, Roman, Anglican, and Lutheran churches.

How are the passages to be selected for reading? In the synagogue they are read serially, the five books of the Law being completely heard in the course of a year. It may be that the Gospels have also been so used, for Mark's Gospel seems to divide into lections. The possibility should not be overlooked. For many centuries, however, the lessons have been chosen selectively, in keeping with a pattern that gives a broad theme to each Sunday within the rhythm of the church seasons. The epistle readings have tended to emphasize the ethical aspects — even the negative ones — of Christian living. Denominations that have not frequently used a lectionary are developing one, and there is a trend toward the development of a two- or three-year lectionary in order to ensure a broad scope for hearing and preaching. There will never be a perfect lectionary, and no matter what a committee finally chooses, there will be ministers and congregations asking why this or that passage was selected. Nevertheless, the value lies in the breadth that can come from a selection designed to have a perspective on the Biblical content, keeping in mind the needs of all the people. It cannot then reflect the interests of a particular minister or the type of reading and preaching desired by one community. It prevents repetition, both of theme and content, and assures continuity.

Protestantism in the past few centuries has laid so much stress on the personal and silent reading of the Bible as almost to lose sight of the particular value in hearing it read. For many centuries this was the only way in which Christians could know the contents of the Bible. Most people were illiterate. Manuscripts were slowly and carefully copied, becoming treasures made by monks as an expression of their vocation and a gift of their talents to the glory of God. They were as highly prized as any other appointment of church and chapel. The invention of printing did not lower the value appreciably, as one realizes in noting that these old Bibles are literally chained to their lecterns. Translations into vernacular languages brought about the possibility of individuals owning portions of a Bible. A growing middle class were sufficiently educated to read for themselves if they were devout and interested. Widespread education, however, is a fairly recent trend, and it is understandable that the Bible should be the most widely distributed but least read of all books. Even in popular paraphrases of the Bible, parts are repetitious, confusing, and obscure. To convey the heart of the Bible's message week by week within the worshiping congregation continues to be the most effective way of making the contents known.

Hearing is still an important avenue of learning. We are being reminded that the " Gutenberg Galaxy " is at a transition point.[18] Today people see and listen, in movies, around television sets, or via radio. This is reminiscent of millennia in which the tradition was passed to each generation through the telling and the hearing of the story. The Bible came into being through an oral tradition. Anything that was written was meant to be read aloud: the Mosaic law, the book of the law that King Josiah found, Jeremiah's letters, or the letters of the apostle Paul.

In order to hear and understand, one must listen. Some people are better able to do this than others. Those whose main form of communication is reading tend to be less apt as listeners. Those who read little tend to be more facile in direct communication. They frequently know how to listen and to hear. For such worshipers as these the Scripture lessons can come alive. A person may also follow the words with his eyes, reading silently while hearing, or reading before or after the service.

The setting is another factor in hearing. The place in which particular words are read influences how they are heard and interpreted. When the Bible is read by an actor at a poetry reading, the audience enjoys the voice, the rhythm, and the interpretation, but does not necessarily hear the meaning addressed personally. When the Bible is read as the introduction to a discussion about it — as might be the case in a Bible-study course — it is heard intellectually in order to seek the meaning in its context, although further meaning might be brought out through the discussion. On Sunday morning the Bible is read in the midst of people who have come together as a congregation because of the day and for the purpose of worshiping God. Hearing the Scriptures becomes part of the total act of worship. The people are in the presence of God and have come to this place for that purpose. (Of course one is in God's presence in other places and at other times, but this is irrelevant at the moment.) The church service is a time when God and his people address each other. Therefore, on this occasion, the Bible is heard specifically as the word through which God is speaking to his people, and as the word through which he has spoken to them. It has personal meaning to each individual, to each congregation, to all Christian congregations wherever they are gathered in all the world on a particular Sunday morning hearing this lesson. There comes a sense of personal communication between the one who reads the lesson and those who hear. Each person in his own way is participating in order that God may be known among his people through the words of Scripture. There is a bond of community among the congregation, for the word is addressed to *all* of them. This is clearly indicated in the letters of Paul, sometimes written to specific congregations, with reference to how those congregations should be witnesses to their Christian faith. Individual messages, greetings from one person to another, are included because they are members of this congregation.

The setting of the worship service includes the place from which the Bible is read, and all the customs that have surrounded the reading emphasize its peculiar importance here. The Bible stands on its own lectern or ambo. To have a separate lectern and pulpit has not always been the custom. Frequently, the connection between the hearing and the interpreting of Scripture has been emphasized by having both words spoken from the same place. Nor has the location of the lectern always been the same. It has been placed at one side of the Communion table (sometimes balanced by the pulpit on the other side). It has been placed on a pulpit behind the table. Some new churches in the Reformed tradition today are seeking ways of giving prominence to both pulpit and table by placing them beside each other as two parts of the same action. At one time, there were two lecterns: one to hold the Gospel, one for the Epistle — from which comes the custom in "liturgical" churches of reading one lesson at each side of the altar. Some churches have brought the Bible to the center front and it is read from there. Each custom in its own way is designed to draw attention to the Book and the reading by having this action alone take place on a particular spot. The "gospel procession" is an expression meaning that the reader picks up the book of the liturgy and carries it either to the lectern or to the center front of the church for reading. In some traditions, it is customary for the congregation to stand during the gospel lesson as the climax of the Scripture readings.

The words that accompany the reading attest to the desire to give it importance. The minister will say, "Hear the word of God as it is contained in . . . ," or, "Here begins . . . ," or after the reading, "May God bless to us the hearing of his Word." There are traditional responses that the congregation makes at the beginning of the gospel, "Glory be to thee, O Lord," and at the close, "Praise be to thee, O Christ." So through various customs, the Christian community has recognized the psychological fact that people come prepared to listen in a certain way in accordance with how they are introduced to what is about to happen. These are not meaningless accretions, cluttering up the Scripture-reading, but ways by which the seriousness of this reading is made known to the people.

The translation in which the Bible is read has its own importance. In the seventeenth century, men died that the

Bible might be translated and made available to people in their own language. Then a tradition began to develop around the classical translation itself, so that it almost became the Word of God to the ears of Christian people. The literati praised its style, but the meaning of the words became more and more obscure. That veneration seems to be nearing its end. The twentieth century has seen numerous retranslations into English, and people are ready to hear fresh statements from the original languages, closer to original meanings and clearer in the use of modern English. It is often less comfortable to hear, especially since the present trend emphasizes the colloquial, and one cannot so readily lose the thrust of the passage in poetic piety.

The immediacy of the Word to all people may sometimes be enhanced when the readers include members of the congregation. No longer is this the same sound — that of the minister's voice — which has already called them to worship, uttered the invocation, and perhaps led in a responsive reading. When a layman leaves his place in the congregation and stands at the lectern to read a lesson, a new voice is introduced and the congregation is conscious of being ministered to by another like themselves. It is an experience to be such a reader, to address one's fellow Christians with the Word of God; it is a serious responsibility to be carefully prepared. If this were taken as a normal procedure, there would be no need for "Laymen's Sunday," "Women's Sunday," and "Young People's Sunday," when each specific age or sex group tends to become performers. Congregations might think about this. Some already have. The custom of reading by a layman is found more frequently in England than in the United States, and is becoming more prevalent in Roman Catholic parishes than in Protestant churches. While Protestants sometimes robe the lay readers (emphasizing participation with clergy and choir), Roman Catholic parishes have preferred to have them come from among the congregation, emphasizing that they represent the laity and that reading the Scripture is part of their responsibility in the worshiping community. The congregation becomes conscious of its service (liturgy) when someone comes forward at the required point, reads from the Bible, and returns to his place.

THE PREACHING

Preaching is an ancient tradition, primarily concerned with interpreting the Scriptures. Because of this function, the practical place for it is immediately following the Scripture-reading. The purpose is to clarify, to explain, and to " make present " the Biblical word. By understanding the historical context, the congregation is placed in the situation of those who first heard it, realizing that God who has acted in the past for his people acts similarly for his people today. Law and gospel are here, judgment and grace. This preaching is for those who belong to Christ — not to awaken faith but to nurture it; hence, it is a teaching function. The good news is proclaimed and brought to bear on specific situations. The Scriptures can become alive in order to be, as they have so often been called, the " living Word."

Such preaching is nurture because it awakens insights. The hearer can begin to see some relationship between these far-off words in the Bible and his own world and personal situation. The Bible reading becomes meaningful now, something more than a difficult passage to be explained and intellectually understood. It has triggered some internal change. As the worshipers listen week after week and year after year attitudes too can change — in individuals, in congregations, even within communities. This has happened. Preaching also strengthens responses, reinforces learning by giving assurance, and reiterates in deeply personal ways the work of God toward men. Although preaching tries to make the Bible intelligible to modern man, it is not primarily dealing with concepts or with religious laws and principles in any abstract way. Even the more didactic passages from the epistles, for instance, were written from within living situations and involved persons. Preaching asks the meaning of the Biblical word for the church then and now.

Missionary preaching (i.e., to nonbelievers) is oriented toward Baptism: it proclaims to those who do not know it the love of God for man in Christ, in the hope that the hearers will accept and respond, and become members of God's people. Liturgical preaching (i.e., performed within the service of worship) is oriented toward the Lord's Supper — toward thanksgiving and participation of the redeemed community in the life of the risen Lord. This accounts for the greater emphasis in such preaching (and in the lessons) on the Christian life and on the witness of Christians in the world. It is not for those who come into the church but for those who go out from its worship.

How long the preaching takes is immaterial. It is more difficult to get at meaning in a few words than to use many. A five-minute sermon would take as careful preparation as a half-hour one. Customs of the times enter here: the medieval homily was brief; the seventeenth-century Puritan sermon was long. It has been getting shorter ever since that time. Protestant worship has laid stress on the sermon as the climax and often the most important part of the service. Here is the word by which the congregation has been fed. This has been a rewarding action for the intellectually inclined or for those who could express themselves emotionally through the hearing of inspirational sermons. Others have found no meaning in lengthy listening and seeming inaction. So Roman Catholic worship, with the dramatic action of the Eucharist, and Pentecostal worship, with the freedom to sing, speak, and move around, have both been more rewarding for the religious expression of people from some cultural backgrounds.

THE LEARNING ABOUT THE BIBLE

There are other ways of learning about the Biblical readings. Some parishes make the lectionary available to their people, encouraging them to use this for individual reading and/or for family worship and study. Some parishes have centered weekly Bible-study groups around the lectionary.[19] Some groups have looked into the background of the passages, using commentaries, and then asked what meaning these words might hold for today. It has even been known that their insights were shared with the minister as he prepared his sermon on the lesson. Some have used a coffee hour after church to explore further the meaning of the Scripture and sermon. This is not a critical evaluation, for the sermon stands in its own right as an authentic part of the service of worship. Such an after-service colloquium assumes that the sermon began to open up the Scripture and that those who gather with the preacher are asking: "What did you mean by this?" "Your saying this reminded me . . ." "Another way in which this speaks is . . ." Here is a place for further sharing which emerges from the worship of the community. Another way of opening up the meaning of the lessons is through a brief note in the calendar, setting out the purpose and main point, and indicating the correlation among the several lessons for the day, especially as these also express the meaning of this day within the liturgical year. Some clergymen give such an introduction orally; others feel that the Scripture should speak for itself.

How the Scripture is read somewhat determines the extent to which it speaks for itself. Any reading is interpretation: a dramatic reading can overinterpret; a monotonous tone suggests meaninglessness. Reading aloud imposes certain obligations on the reader, especially when he is addressing people who usually read for themselves and therefore tend to be eye-minded. He must enunciate clearly, yet read rapidly enough so that the attention does not lag. There must be rhythm and emphasis which clarify meaning. These take practice. Whoever reads, whether clergyman or layman, has an obligation to rehearse his reading aloud in advance so that when he comes to this place in the service, what he reads will be heard and understood. Some readers become anxious (ministers as well as laymen). Suddenly their thoughts and feelings turn in upon themselves. They feel as if they were on exhibition and suspect that they are being judged. (" Suppose I make a mistake — lose the place, repeat a sentence, mispronounce a word? Suppose I cannot be heard by all? Suppose my voice is pitched incorrectly, or I do not enunciate clearly, or I read too fast or too slowly? ") Half-remembered experiences from early childhood reading bedevil one. " I cannot worship when I am leading others in worship," says someone. This anxiety disappears only when one can accept the possibility of reading imperfectly and trust that the rest of the congregation, who also are human, will simply listen along, however one reads. So, forgetting the impression of the self, one can become a member of the congregation participating with others in the worship of God through the reading of the Scriptures.

While the lessons are the main portions of the Bible read in the service, there are several other points at which Scripture carries the liturgy. The call to worship is Biblical; there may be antiphons, versicles, and responses. Some use a reading from The Psalms. Traditionally, this was the " gradual " sung between the gospel and the epistle, and in the Roman liturgy this today consists of several carefully chosen verses from a psalm, different each week. The Psalter links the Christian church with earlier synagogue worship. The offertory sentences are Biblical, as is one traditional offertory response: " All things come of thee, O Lord. . . ." The benediction is Biblical. The Lord's Supper always includes the words of institution, usually from

First Corinthians. So the service of worship moves from point to point, using the language of the Bible, and always in a new way, as it enhances and makes plain the worship of God.

The Bible heard and preached is an integral element in the service of worship, but as the individual takes part week by week he is learning much and its use becomes educational. He learns the story that the Bible tells, and he learns what it says to him for his life as a Christian in today's world. He learns by hearing — listening to what is read. He learns by seeing — caught up in the presence of God expressed through the words of this Book read from its special place, heard and responded to. He learns by doing — the action of his voice and body when he responds in Biblical verses as he stands or sits to hear. He learns as he understands and accepts within himself some of the meanings that the Bible holds, for the Bible is the book of God's community and it holds words of joyful assurance. Thus the hearing of the Scriptures is an indispensable part of Christian worship.

| CHAPTER 4 | PRAYER IN WORSHIP |

PRAYER IS AT THE HEART of any personalized religion. Not all forms of religion require this. One can believe that God exists but define him as essentially an impersonal force. One can hold a "religion of mankind" and strive to fulfill to the highest one's humanity. God made known in the Bible is affirmed as the living God — a God who acts through events; who addresses particular men; who calls a people; who loves, judges, saves. Verbs alone can describe him. Personal interaction is his mode of revelation. Hence the medieval categories, derived from Greco-Roman philosophizing, which tried to describe God in adjectives and nouns — omnipotence, omniscience, omnipresence, aseity, etc. — may provide a different way of thinking about God, but are little help in developing the Biblical categories of description.

Prayer is derived from the Biblical thinking about God, and the forms of prayer spring from the ways in which Biblical people addressed God. Their prayers were varied. They blessed and thanked him; they confessed their sinfulness and unworthiness; they petitioned him for many needs; they rebuked him and questioned his call and his actions; they called upon him to destroy their enemies. They were completely honest in their speech with God.

This indicates that they trusted him: they knew that they could not hide from him, for he knew them better than they knew themselves. They also knew that he was the Holy One, so there was no use in trying to pretend that they were good. He had called them, made a covenant with them; they were his people, so there was no need to fear him. This was a solid basis for relationship. Liturgical prayer was more formal, more careful, for it lifted before God the petitions of the whole people. These were remembrances of what God had done, recited as prelude to the petition for his present blessing; for example, Psalm 136 or the words of Solomon at the dedication of the Temple (II Chron. 6:13 f.). Biblical prayer was a dialogue: man had heard himself addressed by God, and his prayer was the response to God, whether in praise, in protest, or in petition.

The service of worship is basically the action of a congregation in dialogue with God. It is responsive in nature. The opening is praise and adoration, expressed in words of Scripture, hymn, and invocation. God's people address him at the opening of an act of communal worship. Next they listen, addressed by him in the words of Scripture, explicated in sermon. Again they respond, in faith and trust making known their petitions. They offer to God their needs, they offer their money — which represents their life — they offer themselves in perpetual dedication as they go out into the " world."

Congregational worship suggests both the form and content for personal devotion. From participation in this action the individual finds a norm that can deepen and enlarge the daily prayer. The intercessions help him to become aware of how wide are the world's needs and prevent him from centering his concern on the self and the persons immediate to him. The joy of praise and thanksgiving give him a perspective on which to lay hold even in darkest moments. And in the times when, for various reasons, prayer seems empty or impossible, the weekly participation in the prayer of the church holds him faithful in the presence of God, who cares and who understands even that which remains unexpressed.

PRAYER IN CORPORATE WORSHIP

Corporate worship in all its words and actions is addressed to God, and this includes prayer. Hymns, psalms, and canticles at the opening are joyous addresses which praise and bless him, whether it be " Now Thank We All Our God," the Gloria in Excelsis, or verses from The Psalms. As has already been suggested, the term now coming into general use with reference to the Lord's Supper is " Eucharist," which means " thanksgiving," and the opening phrase of the canon is " We give thanks unto thee." The action ends with a thanksgiving. This is the mood for Christian worship.

Thanksgiving alone, however, would not express the deepest meanings of prayer. We say " thank you " spontaneously to anyone who is responsible for that which we have experienced as good or helpful. There is no need here for a personal relationship. It can be simply a gesture of courtesy. Relationship is expressed only when we can ask for help and confess weakness. This is true for human relationships; it is true for the relationship with God. This is the basic thesis for Friedrich Heiler's classic exposition of the subject.[20] To ask another is to expose oneself, to become vulnerable. A person does this only if he trusts the other, if he believes that he is loved for himself (and not for what he does) . Such prayer precludes fear; one can indeed petition (beg) from fear, but one cannot love and therefore establish a mutual relationship. The person who loves and is sure of being loved does not hesitate to ask. The assurance of acceptance makes honesty possible. When this is applied to the prayer of the whole congregation, it further implies a mutual acceptance of one another and a sensitivity to another's needs before God. If a congregation is to avail itself of the sustaining power of mutual prayer for any member in need, it must so love each member that anyone dares to admit his need. If the congregation is to pray that God will act in the tragic needs of this world, it must be sensitive to the varied ways in which its own people react to those needs. Neither God nor the congregation can be pressured. Prayer is not magic. God is not coerced. From one side, this means that he who prays cannot expect that what he wants will be done. The New Testament is clear on this: " Let it be to me according to your word " is Mary's acceptance of the difficult divine task laid upon her; " Not as I will, but as thou wilt," prays Jesus in the Garden of Gethsemane. From the other side, one need not draw the conclusion that it is needless to pray because God knows all man's needs and desires. This neglects the active role which man plays in God's creation (" have dominion over . . .") and in his redemption (called and sent). Because God acts, man can pray. He acts through people, which is why petition has its place. Praying men are the channels through whom God's purposes can be fulfilled in the world.

To believe that all prayer is fulfilled in some way and that all of God's actions are in some ultimate way good is not rationalizing or evading the tragic aspects of life. Rather, it is an acceptance that tragedy is written into the fabric of existence, that life is difficult, that redemption and re-creation have to do with bringing something good out of evil. This is a mystery, but it is fulfilled again and again, as many can testify. Sometimes good can emerge only when an evil is brought to light. So it is necessary that the Christian congregation in prayer face the evil in life, and yield themselves to God for the healing of the world's ills. He has promised to be with them and to empower them, and they, presumably, trust him. By enunciating the petition in concrete terms, people see the need more clearly. They are also faced with the necessity of finding some form of action in which they can engage, since they do not believe that God waves a wand to intervene, but know that he has called them to carry out this purpose. Beyond this, however, there are times when prayer is the only form of action one can take. There is a necessary emotional release in having a channel through which to express one's fears and concerns and then be able to rest quietly in the assurance that in time some positive action will occur. Patience is a part of prayer; God's time does not go by man's clock.

The prayer of the congregation may be expressed in several forms. Protestant services have usually included all petitions under one pastoral prayer, which is carefully prepared by the pastor, aware that he is leading his people. Some traditions have used a series of collects, each expressing a specific area of need, each affirmed by the congregation with a vocal " Amen."

The collect is a specific form, much as poetry has specific form. Beginning with an address to God, and an ascription about him, it continues with a petition and the hoped-for result, and ends, " in the name of Jesus." For example:

O God, who makest us glad with the weekly remembrance of the glorious resurrection of thy Son our Lord; Vouchsafe us this day such blessing through our worship of thee, that the days to come may be spent in thy service; through the same Jesus Christ our Lord. Amen.[21]

Another specific form is that of the litany. This is a series of petitions, to each of which the people respond with a sentence such as " We pray thee to hear us, O Lord," or a variant of the same. In a congregation trained in the work of prayer, such petitions would have been submitted by individuals to the leader of worship in advance so that the prayer could proceed without hesitation or awkwardness. In a small group, petitions could be voiced by individuals, with everyone affirming the prayer in the response. For example:

> For the forgiveness of our sins through which we have caused pain to our neighbors, tempted others to anger, and separated ourselves from thee,
> *We pray thee to hear us, O Lord.*
> That the hunger of working men, nourishing mothers, and all children be relieved in places of poverty and famine, as in India, Brazil, and areas of our cities,
> *We pray thee to hear us, O Lord.*
> That we may understand what it means to live under judgment and accept the tasks of redeeming grace made known to us through generations of the experiences of thy community,
> *We pray thee to hear us, O Lord.*

The advantage of either collects or litany over the pastoral prayer is simply that the prayer is broken into small sections and the people are constantly affirming the words by their own voices and participating verbally as well as mentally.[22]

The one prayer that Christians have been able to use in unison has been the Lord's Prayer. So important has this been in the life of the worshiping community that many books on the subject of prayer seem to derive from it and to be explications of or meditations on it. The New Testament setting is that of a prayer which Jesus gave to his disciples. In Matthew's Gospel it is placed in the Sermon on the Mount, as part of a teaching about prayer; in Luke's Gospel it follows a request of one of the disciples who had observed Jesus in prayer, " Lord, teach us to pray." In the light of this presumed origin, it is most appropriate that the prayer should be used when his people are gathered together for worship. (And it is not appropriate for indiscriminate community gatherings of people.) The Lord's Prayer, in brief form, is a summation of the needs of God's people. The Matthean form ends with a doxology, generally used by Protestants and usually omitted by Roman Catholics. It is a fitting close to the specific prayers of the congregation. In the Eucharistic service it is usually placed just before the people approach the table. A place could well be made in the service for more unison prayers, such as saying together a collect for the day and using together a concluding thanksgiving.

Silence is another avenue for prayer, whether it be a wordless openness toward God or an inward voicing of speech. The moments after the arrival at the service are for preparation. Here silence can lead to words; the words of the opening hymn can suggest thoughts: prayers from a book of worship can be an aid. It is not wise to brush aside the use of all prayers previously written as somehow being inferior to one's immediate thoughts. Sometimes another person, versed in the life of devotion, can express thoughts in words which hold the worshiper deeply within the presence of God. A congregation could be helped by having such prayers made available for use. The silence at the offertory suggests meditation on the sermon and a silent offering of oneself to God. The silence at the Communion is an opportunity also for self-offering and for thanksgiving. The silence as the service draws to an end suggests that one's thoughts turn toward the world outside. There is strength received in common worship; the grace of God, asked for and received in faith, goes with his people as they leave that assemblage. The offering of the self to God is not a once-and-for-all event, but is daily renewed alone and weekly renewed in the congregation. One is particularly conscious of this at the time of the offering and at the close of the service.

PRAYER AS PERSONAL DEVOTION

Prayer is not confined to the sanctuary, even if it takes its direction from that event. God is known in aloneness or he is never fully known (insofar as human beings can know him). This is the moment of truth. It is a waste of time simply to utter words. It deceives the self and insults God, who makes himself available to all his children. The Biblical word concerning God's understanding of man is stated in Psalm 139:

> Thou discernest my thoughts from afar.
> Thou searchest out my path and my lying
>   down,
>   and art acquainted with all my ways.
> Even before a word is on my tongue,
>   lo, O Lord, thou knowest it altogether.
> Thou dost beset me behind and before,
>   and layest thy hand upon me.
> Such knowledge is too wonderful for me;
>   it is high, I cannot attain it.
>
> (Vs. 2-6.)

This is a good beginning for anyone's prayer. It sets one on a straight path. No point is gained by laboring under illusions. God would not be God if he did not know a person better than parent or spouse knows him. It is useless to lie to God. In kindness it must be said that most people do not consciously do this; they have first lied to themselves. Holding the self to an impossible ideal, they cannot admit to themselves the impossibility of fulfillment. Two possibilities are open: to condemn other people who are worse; to excuse one's own shortcomings or reinterpret them. It is only human to fall into some such trap. So the beginning of prayer is a searching knowledge of the self, a task in which one can be sure that God helps by loving the person for himself and not for his performance. (Those who love others for their performance are unable to grasp this; they are already under judgment.) The love (grace) of God is freely offered, not to give false securities or easy forgiveness, but in order to make it possible for the worshiper to bear the pain of seeing the self and knowing its needs. Only then can the new work of upbuilding begin. A wound must be opened and cleansed before it can be healed. Otherwise, it will fester and even cause death.

Words are the symbols that human beings use in communication. They do not necessarily reveal; as often as not they conceal real meaning. They can also become a barrier against feeling. Feelings lie deeper than words. This is why it is possible to pray without words, and in moments of inexpressible joy or uncontrollable distress, silence is the only form of communication. Feelings can also be negative: anxiety, hostility. People sometimes fail to realize that to be anxious is to feel threatened, and to feel threatened is to have anger, i.e., hostility, aroused. Those who believe that God loves them can acknowledge in his presence both the fears and the anger and thereby find the possibility of solution, which is wholeness. God cleanses; he heals. The healing narratives in the Gospels attest to this.

So there is indeed a chain of prayer. Trust leads to openness of the self which makes possible real confession; this leads to the realization and acceptance of God's forgiveness. Now the self and others can be seen anew. One can pray for the needs of the world, of others, of the self, of friends and enemies. One does not pray in spite of feelings but because of feelings — renewed, turned around, converted. When one is released into joy, there comes the time for praise and thanksgiving — to bless God for his wonderful works toward the children of men.

Christians today often find the subject of prayer, and the practicing of it, awkward and uncomfortable. This was clearly brought out at a conference of church workers who admitted their own discomfort when asked to participate in small prayer groups. What was happening there? A psychiatrically trained leader suggested that while people from simple cultural and educational backgrounds could participate in such a group on a quite personal, even naïve, level, their leaders from sophisticated educational backgrounds found (although they could scarcely admit this to themselves) that the gathering just did not make sense. From early childhood they had been exposed to a culture geared to the scientific measure, to the assurance of a cause-and-effect universe, to reality as that which could be grasped through symbol or concept if not in physical fact. Yet here were people speaking aloud in the presence of others to a Being whom they could not see, yet who " saw " them, who had not ears but could " hear " them, who spoke no language but understood all languages, who helped some people without hurting others. This was beyond all practical imagination. Theoretically, they accepted, i.e., believed; but this particular event was unbelievable. Prayer in the context of Sunday worship was different. There was form and sequence; there was historical precedent; there was a " controlled " situation; spontaneity was at a minimum and so was uncertainty. Doubts could be accommodated, questions distributed.

How shall one speak in this situation? A perceptive article by John B. Coburn (who had written earlier on the subject of prayer) takes up the challenge of current theological ferment in relation to this perplexing area of Christian experience. Starting from the comments on prayer by John A. T. Robinson, in *Honest to God*,[23] Dean Coburn discusses the following ideas:

The world shapes the spiritual. The spiritual life is expressed, therefore, in the world as well as in the church. Spiritual guidance will come from the " friends of God " in the world rather than exclusively from the church. Materials for meditation are provided by the world where men live now.[24]

He suggests that these changes in personal prayer seem to be taking place:

The central prayer is the affirmation of one's own being within the context of his personal situation — with thanksgiving. Confession includes not simply one's specific sins, but what one is as a whole man. Petition and intercession are thought of not only in terms of what God can do, but what man can do. There is a trend to simplicity (ignoring traditional "progress" in prayer). A Christian style of spirituality stresses the immediacy of a response to God and recognizes that it may be hidden. There is no universal way to prayer.

At the same time, Dean Coburn raises questions about some of the stresses in contemporary thinking.

1. Real life requires not only engagement in the world but also withdrawal, solitude, disengagement.

2. The emphasis upon God as immanent could neglect his transcendence.

3. Is not the idea of a personal God who enters upon a personal encounter with persons denied?

4. Can spirituality ever be developed without some acceptance of ascesis?

5. Are we not in fact faced in our generation with a crisis in belief rather than a crisis in formulations of belief? Doubt may be the form of the cross for this day. By sharing the unbelief of the world, we can affirm our faith in " the God of hope." [25]

Prayer requires openness. The world today is one of uncertainty, in which no real security or sense of permanence is to be found. Why, then, should the believer expect to have all the answers to prayer or receive all the answers from prayer? No proof can ever be had for faith, trust, love, hope — human or divine. These exist in human hearts simply from the necessity that they be. Life experiences negate them as often as affirming them, but still they persist. So it is with man's personal relationship to the unseen yet ever-present God. Neither signs nor proofs will be given. Deep relationships neither develop nor persevere because of them. The European theologian Hans Urs von Balthasar writes:

Prayer is a dialogue, not a monologue recited by men in God's presence. Indeed there is really no such thing as solitary speech; speech is essentially mutual, a sharing of thoughts and minds, union in a common spirit, in a shared truth. Speech supposes an I and a Thou, and is their mutual manifestation. What do we do, when at prayer, but speak to a God who long ago revealed himself to man in a word so powerful and all-embracing that it can never be solely of the past, but continues to resound through the ages? The better we learn to pray, the more we are convinced that our halting utterance to God is but an answer to God's speech to us; and so it is only in God's language that we can commune with him. God spoke first — and only because he has thus " exteriorized " himself can man " interiorize " himself towards God.[26]

EDUCATION FOR PRAYER

There is an education for prayer which the Christian community offers to one another. It begins with participation in the prayer of the liturgy, week by week. To this, everyone — child and adult — is bidden. How can the child learn to mature in prayer if he has no opportunity to participate in mature prayer? There are other settings for group participation, a church school class or various forms of family worship such as the blessing before the family meal and the child's evening prayer. Participation with others lends a pattern, gives forms, suggests intentions, and makes possible inclusiveness as the concerns of the congregation are sustained in the prayer of individual members during the week.

Learning comes through identification with leaders well versed in prayer. A whole attitude is revealed in tone of voice, words, and manner. Some well-meaning leaders use what seems like an artificial pitch, which is neither sung nor spoken; some use a rhythm peculiar to this purpose. Some ramble in many directions with no apparent pattern of thought; others seem to be preaching to the people through God; some repeat the address to God continuously from sentence to sentence; some use " you " and " thou " forms — and even the third person singular — interchangeably. This suggests to the hearer that it does not matter how one addresses God; that carefulness and precision are not important. It suggests a familiarity brought through carelessness and ignores the fact that the address to God might be as carefully considered as the address to any human person. Leaders in informal prayer groups are sometimes hesitant to the point of arousing anxiety on the part of other participants, or they may be personal to the point of discomfiture in their petitions. What kind of identification is being made here by children or young people who listen and mentally repeat the words, by new people who are not well versed in the forms of prayer? This suggests the seriousness of the task. Informality is not familiarity; spontaneity is not carelessness. The thoughtful leader who is sensitive to the meaning of his action in the religious development of others will be careful in these areas.

Participation in congregational worship gives a pattern for personal devotion and suggests possibilities for deepening. The person who week by week is involved in common worship finds his vocabulary enriched by word and phrase from hymns, Scripture, and the prayers used in the service. He finds his concerns enlarged, especially if the service itself voices praise, thanksgiving, and intercession with a deep understanding of the meaning of creation and redemption. There is an interaction between common worship and personal devotion wherein each strengthens the other and neither can be neglected without harm to the other. The hymnbook and the service book are sources for devotional literature, and the worshiper would find it helpful to use one of them as he sits quietly in the church during the prelude. The same words will be equally helpful when he is alone. Some of the words of the Psalter were originally written as individual prayers, and the modern worshiper will find them still helpful. Psalms 23 and 46 are well-known affirmations of trust; Psalm 139 is a penetrating prayer of confession and assurance. Nor should one overlook a section in most hymnals with suggested material for worship, including brief prayers for thanksgiving, confession, and petition.

A false division is sometimes made between spontaneous prayer and the use of previously written prayers, with the assumption that spontaneity makes the former qualitatively superior to the latter. Superior to whom? Or why? Those who out of a deep relationship to God have written down the words from their hearts and preserved them to be shared with others have given a treasury for which succeeding generations owe thanks. They are the teachers and guides to others who may in turn do likewise. To pray in the words of another is not to do so falsely, but rather in deep truth, having found words to express what the heart has felt. No one should despise the help that another gives, but instead rejoice in it. Sometimes such prayers are used along with spontaneous words. Sometimes they form the beginning for meditation. Sometimes they speak so meaningfully as to be memorized and used again and again. The Bible speaks of " knowing" God, using this term in a deep and intimate sense. If this is accepted, then the fullness of " knowing " can deepen across the years only in those who are free enough to explore the many avenues of knowing, realizing that one's own ways of expression will also change. The formal, the colloquial, the written, the spontaneous, the inward speech, and the silence are all ways of expressing this relationship of " knowing." The omission of any one element impoverishes the expression of the relationship. How unfortunate to be inhibited on this point by training or tradition!

Whether to memorize particular prayers or not is an individual matter. Those which are used week after week

in the congregation are memorized by use. One participates as a member of the worshiping congregation. Such
familiarity can induce a monotonous repetition, but need
not do so. On the contrary, knowing the words inwardly
can release the worshiper to absorb and express the meaning that they have for him. The Lord's Prayer is the classical expression of prayer used throughout Christendom.
However, the congregation which has only this one avenue
of communal prayer is deprived. New liturgies, as they become widely known, give opportunities for all to join in
other words of thanksgiving and intercession. The grace
said by a family before a meal unites this group before
God, continuing an ancient custom which even the pagans
used (recalling the apostle Paul's words to Christians concerned about eating food offered to idols). This thanksgiving could be said in unison or spoken by one member.
It could be spontaneous or learned from the traditional
ones available and include one or more written by a family
for its own use. In personal devotion an individual might
find one prayer of deep meaning which would be used
daily for a period of time, perhaps later to be joined by or
replaced with another.

Education in prayer comes also through direct teaching.
Many books have been written on the meaning of the
Lord's Prayer. When children first learn it (as they usually
do around the age of six whether one agrees to this educationally or not), they need to be helped to understand
something of its meaning. They are receiving enough instruction in reading at school to enable them to recognize
words. The phrases of the prayer can be printed on the
bulletin board or chalkboard and the class given time to
see, hear, read aloud, and talk about what each phrase is
saying in terms that are meaningful for their lives. The
value lies in giving the children a vocal part in morning
worship when they are attending. Adults will find this a
fruitful area for study through small groups, and the

prayer will surely be used from time to time in preaching. Teaching specific forms of prayer is another means of education in devotion. Little children can learn and use the litany form. Traditionally, this is a prayer of intercession, but modern usage has broadened it to include responses, which can make it a prayer of thanksgiving. Such a litany can gather the thoughts of a group at the conclusion of a unit of study as members of the class add their phrases orally or in written form. Sometimes a litany is written out for each member to be able to keep and use. A class activity may involve making a book of prayers to be used at home, for individual or family use, perhaps during some special time of year such as Lent. A class might also develop for home use a service of worship for a special day, such as Thanksgiving, Christmas Eve, New Year's Day, Easter, or a birthday. Collects have a precision that commend them to adults, also to children at an age when they like to construct. Individually and as a group, fifth-graders and those older can fill in the outlines of the form to voice a concern, for this is essentially petitionary prayer. Familiarity comes with practice. Each week for a given period of time one member of the class could be asked to open the session, using a collect of his own or one from an outside source so that the rhythm becomes familiar. The sequence is already familiar from attendance at morning worship when the form is regularly used there. The practice needed is in using the form orally and in writing. Learning comes not only by composition but by using the form aloud in leading a group in worship. This can be done with older boys and girls, young people, and adults. No one should ever be pressured into such participation, for some find it difficult. Complete openness to the possibility that some will and some will not participate should always be the frame of reference of the leader.

Learning in prayer also takes place through participation in small groups meeting together for this purpose.

They have usually been ongoing groups which find open-ness in mutual support. Indeed, there is a danger that a prayer group will develop a closed membership into which new members cannot enter. Unlike many "contract" groups which meet for a definite period of study and then disband, the devotional group, even if it starts in this way, will frequently elect to stay together. This can be good, provided it does not become ingrown. Such a group will share together comments from the reading of devotional books, both new and old. They will find the life of prayer enriched by Biblical study, particularly of passages chosen for this purpose, and through the use of Biblical prayers (there are some moving ones in the epistles). They grow through the use with one another of sustaining silence and in sharing intercession vocally.

Further training includes learning how to use silence. This puzzles some, because silence in the sense of becoming mentally blank, although cultivated and practiced in East-ern religious life, is not a Western mode of expression. Meditation in Western devotion has more form and does include thought. It is introspective and makes use of free association, which then centers down to a focus. External disturbances are better recognized and accepted, in a sense "prayed into" the devotion so that they cease to be the obstruction they can be through the conscious effort to ignore them: voices outside, the hum of traffic, the ticking of a clock, the sound of a distant radio. This attitude can be taught. The bidding prayer is an avenue for beginning to learn (and can be used even with young children, al-though most frequently associated with youth and adults). "Let us pray for . . . ," bids the leader, thereafter allow-ing an appropriate moment of silence. How long the "mo-ment" is reflects the skill of the leader as teacher, for the leader must be relaxed, able to sense the silence and the feeling of the group, knowing when, in the course of weeks together, the silence can be lengthened. One of the possible barriers to the development of the receptive use of silence is the assumption that silence must be engaged in with closed eyes and bowed head. This is sensed at the close of morning worship when people await the extinguishing of candles or the close of a quiet organ interval, succeeded by the crashing opening chords of a postlude that practically raises them to their feet. To sit quietly contemplating the cross, the Communion table, the Bible, reredos, window, carving, or whatever symbol toward which the attention is directed, encourages the use of silence. " How long " is an individual matter; the silence of each sustains everyone in whatever way that silence is observed.

Little children can learn to appreciate the use of silence. Adults need it. Sometimes one needs first to learn the process of relaxing sufficiently to receive. The awareness that God speaks through the undirected thought to bring new insight, a new way of looking at oneself and one's situation, a new integration of understanding, can be accepted only through openness — physical, mental, emotional. The recall of particular persons or of specific situations calls forth a centering of concern and leads to the words and phrases formed in specific petition. The church should be able to offer this kind of learning to people.

The need to pray may lie deep within the human person, but praying is a learned response. Skill grows with knowledge and with use, but the deepening is essential to an ever fuller relationship with the living God.

| CHAPTER 5 | MUSIC IN WORSHIP |

S INGING HAS LONG BEEN an integral part of worship in the Biblical tradition. It is written that when the people of Israel had safely fled the pursuing Egyptians across the Red Sea, " then Moses and the people of Israel sang this song to the Lord " (Ex. 15:1) , and there follows the ancient hymn of victory praising God who has saved his people. The completion of the retelling of the law in the book of Deuteronomy is closed with another " song of Moses," praising God who is faithful and just and who will bring judgment on his people if they stray from him. Deborah's song and David's song are songs of deliverance. Modern worshipers might be startled by the picture given by the Chronicler of that fateful pilgrimage made in the hope of bringing the Ark to Jerusalem when " David and all Israel were making merry before God with all their might, with song and lyres and harps and tambourines and cymbals and trumpets " (I Chron. 13:8) . Hezekiah, on becoming king, repaired the Temple and held a service of rededication at which he " commanded the Levites to sing praises to the Lord with the words of David and of Asaph the seer. And they sang praises with gladness, and they bowed down and worshiped " (II Chron. 29:30) .

In the New Testament we read that Jesus and his disciples, after their last supper, sang a hymn, probably one of the psalms appointed for the Passover season. The first Christian generation were told to " be filled with the Spirit, addressing one another in psalms and hymns and spiritual songs, singing and making melody to the Lord with all your heart " (Eph. 5:18-19).

Beyond simple references to singing, there is a great body of verse in the Bible. The Psalms are a particularly rich source for religious songs, variously called psalms, canticles, or hymns. The Psalms contain songs of various types, some for personal use, and some more appropriate for the use of choirs and of assemblies of praise.

The pilgrimage is of ancient origin, and the people, as they traveled, beguiled the hours with religious marching songs, recounting the purpose of their travel. Similar songs continued to be used in Europe during the popular pilgrimages that took place in the late Middle Ages and the Renaissance period. Young people today are known to enliven the hours with pilgrim songs of their own while going toward their destination by bus or plane. The Freedom Marches brought a new flowering of pilgrimage songs that combine the rhythm for walking, an affirmation of faith in the task, narratives concerning the work, and words for mutual encouragement.

The New Testament has its own songs echoing early Christian worship. These were not apparent to the general reader until new translations began to set them apart in verse lines that stress their rhythm. Such are Mary's song, Simeon's song, and Zechariah's song, all of which were later incorporated into the monastic offices and survive today among the canticles in *The Book of Common Prayer* or in anthem settings. So also is the Sanctus (Rev. 4:8 and Isa. 6:3) which has been preserved for use at the opening of the Eucharistic banquet in the Orthodox, Roman, and Anglican rites and is now being restored in other traditions.

THE DEVELOPMENT OF HYMNODY

Present hymnals trace the entire history of the development of Christian song, both words and music. One hymnal lists a second-century Passiontide hymn by Clement of Alexandria as its oldest and includes also two third-century Greek hymns. Palm Sunday's familiar " All Glory, Laud, and Honor " comes from the ninth century, and Easter's " Come, Ye Faithful, Raise the Strain of Triumphant Gladness " was written by John of Damascus in the eighth century. " O Come, O Come, Emmanuel " is a tenth-century hymn, and " O Sacred Head, Now Wounded " comes from the twelfth century. The Reformation brought a new flowering of hymnody. Martin Luther has given both " A Mighty Fortress Is Our God " and the Christmas carol " From Heaven High I Come to You." By the fifteenth century, hymns can be dated specifically and the names of the writers are frequently known. Philipp Nicolai in the sixteenth century wrote the familiar Advent hymn " Sleepers, Awake " and the Epiphany hymn " How Bright Appears the Morning Star." The Moravians enriched the hymnal with the devotional poetry of their hymns as well as by their sturdy chorale tunes.

The Genevan Reformation brought psalm paraphrases that became the normative hymnody for the Continental Calvinists, the Scottish Presbyterians, the English Reformed tradition (both established and dissenting), and the American Puritan tradition. Louis Bourgeois' tune " Old Hundredth " has come down in its original form and in many settings, including the familiar Doxology and William Kethe's English rendering (1561) of Ps. 100, " All People That on Earth Do Dwell." The eighteenth century brought Isaac Watts's smoother rendering of psalms as in " O God, Our Help in Ages Past," and later the incomparable hymns of Charles Wesley, such as " Hark! the Herald Angels Sing" and " ' Christ the Lord Is Risen Today.' "

Nineteenth-century hymnody is still being sifted. Its words are popular, and some, such as Reginald Heber's " Holy, Holy, Holy! Lord God Almighty! " are Biblically enough oriented to have a strong possibility for survival. The nineteenth century is the Romantic period in poetry, novel, music, art — and naturally reflects this in its hymnody, which tends to be subjective, inward, personal. The early twentieth century brought an emphasis on hymns for the social gospel, such as Frank Mason North's " Where Cross the Crowded Ways of Life," and found a culmination in Harry Emerson Fosdick's " God of Grace and God of Glory," written for the dedication of The Riverside Church in New York City, and now successfully wedded to a strong Welsh tune. Each new edition of a hymnal brings a few written contemporaneously, and since several hymnals are soon scheduled for publication, the stress of hymnody in the late twentieth century can be assessed. The Introduction of one hymnal estimates that the average life of a hymnal is twenty-five years, after which the process of review and renewal begins.

The earliest music in the hymnals is plainsong, some examples of which have survived from the sixth century. This is a method of speaking on one tone, with the pauses at the end of a phrase indicated by a drop in the tone. It is easy to sing because the words take precedence over the music, and the musical phrase is repeated throughout the hymn. Until recently, the lack of precise time and meter and the use of the minor mode have made plainsong seem strange to ears accustomed to the melodies of the Romantic era. Twentieth-century music, however, has in large part been based on the twelve-tone scale and to people brought up with this, plainsong does not sound strange. It is being used anew by church composers, especially in France, and recordings from the daily offices as sung by the Protestant monks at Taizé are becoming familiar. Father Gelineau's settings for the psalms have successfully found the cadence for carrying the psalms in French, and the English translation indicates that his music fits this language equally well.

The earliest melodic music to be found in the hymnal is in fourteenth-century settings for Christmas carols such as "Good Christian Men, Rejoice." The Reformation brought distinctive music in the form of the chorale and the Genevan psalm tune. The eighteenth century saw the rise of more melodic tunes, with freer meter, and this trend continued into the nineteenth century. Along the way, melodies by great composers from Palestrina to Healey Willan have made a contribution. Sometimes there have been in use thinly-veiled adaptations from operatic arias, but a new note of simplicity is developing in church music. A distinction should be made between spiritual songs used for mutual strengthening and the music of the liturgy offered before God in worship.

How Music Is Used

All types of hymns have found their place in the service of worship. Psalms are often read or sung responsively. When not so used, they have survived as selected verses to link parts of the service: the introit or entrance song, the gradual between the two Scripture readings, and the offertory. The psalms have been set to varied types of music, and plainsong is the closest form of ancient music extant. In Protestant usage, the measured rhythm of common time ($\frac{4}{4}$) in the Genevan and Scottish psalm tunes was the setting used by the Calvinist tradition. The words were rigidly fixed to meter and "lined out" for singing without accompaniment. Because of this construction for *a cappella* use, psalm tunes are easier to learn than are later melodies, for a strong first line carries the tune and is repeated with only slight modification. This makes it similar to the more ancient forms of chant. The Church of England developed its own form of chants for psalm settings when the psalms were translated from Latin into English. In contemporary forms, the meaning of the words is emphasized and the music becomes a simple accompaniment. It is possible so to concentrate on learning a melody that the meaning of the words is lost. Even when the words are read responsively, this can happen if attention becomes more focused on the alternation of speaking than on the meaning of the phrases read. Leaders of worship often do not realize that such reading needs practice if the congregation is to become aware that this is a mutual choric reading of praise.

Early Christian hymns have survived in the daily offices, specifically in Morning Prayer and Evening Prayer of the Anglican churches. They have also been used by composers as the settings for choir anthems. Several other early hymns have become permanently attached to the Eucharistic service, including the Gloria in Excelsis and the Kyrie. The Sanctus introduces the thanksgiving as the hymn of praise sung by minister and people; the Agnus Dei has preceded the Communion. Doxologies are usually attached to the classic musical setting of Louis Bourgeois' "Praise God from Whom All Blessings Flow."

Basically, the purpose of hymnody is the praise of God, and the Biblical forms fulfill this purpose. Another purpose of hymnody seems to have been that of mutual strengthening and encouragement. This is what the pilgrim hymns do, or the songs sung by the persecuted. Songs can enunciate fundamental understandings, such as affirming one's trust in God or describing what it means to live as a Christian. Although Protestant hymnals have a large share of such hymns, congregations have not understood clearly their place and purpose. The classification of three hymns in a service as successively voicing praise, prayer, and dedication needs rethinking. If morning worship is construed as a time of praise, there is need of a larger proportion of such hymns for this service. The hymns of assurance, affirmation, or dedication have more place in other settings such as devotional services at special times. The Sunday evening and midweek services for several generations gave ample scope for the development and use of such hymns, which may be a reason why present hymnals still include so large a number of them. The special events held in Lent, including Holy Week, give such an opportunity. Advent and Christmas gatherings give a similar opportunity. One remembers a Sunday evening gathering to which the choir invited the congregation. All sat around small tables in the dining room. Alternately, the choir sang the unusual carols they had prepared for the season and then joined with the assembled group in singing the more familiar ones. The " Service of Lessons and Carols " now becoming popular is another occasion for the use of varied carols. The lessons for Christmastide alternate with the carols. Part of the tradition is that the first lesson is read by a small child, the successive readers increasing in age until the elders of the congregation (chronologically and responsibly) become involved. Good Friday services provide another opportunity for using devotional hymns. Here is where " O Sacred Head, Now Wounded " and other chorales, as well as some of the medieval music, come into their own. Prayer groups will sometimes share the use of meditative hymns. Family nights and devotional services preceding a school of religion could also provide a place for such hymns.

Some hymns are more meaningful when read without music. This is because they were originally written as devotional poetry, later being set to music. The practice of singing prayers is a tradition within Protestant worship, otherwise devoid of unison prayers with the single exception of the Lord's Prayer. Perhaps an increasing use of unison confession and thanksgiving, and of litanies and " Amens " would lessen the necessity for this choice. Frequently, such a prayer hymn is used as a response, or after the pastoral prayer, or at the close of the service, seeming to indicate a need for additional communal prayer. It has sometimes been a custom to have the choir sing such a response, and even the "Amens," but this takes from the whole congregation a responsibility that they need for their own full participation in worship.

There was a period in American hymnody that stressed didactic hymns, not affirmations of Christian living but attempts to tell people how they should live. People can learn, at least verbally, through words set to music, as is indicated by the use of "singing commercials" on radio and television. This forms a slogan type of learning that combines repetition (words) with emotion (tune) and does not require internalization. This kind of hymn finds little place in recent hymnals. Quite different in purpose is a hymn that expresses sheer joyous witness, such as "O for a thousand tongues to sing my great Redeemer's praise." Many of Charles Wesley's hymns and numerous sixteenth-century Continental hymns set to choral tunes also fit this category.

OTHER FORMS FOR MUSIC

Organ music has been acceptable in most of Christendom, although there are and have been groups that eschewed its use — the early Puritans as well as some smaller groups today. Descended from the wind instruments with which the early Hebrews praised the Lord, the present-day organ is decidedly less portable. People tend to think of it as providing "mood music" or a way to cover up silence. No professional organist would agree. The organ music itself is praise and offering. The prelude and postlude (each a different type of music) help the worshiper to enter into the service of worship by a direct and intelligible involvement as he follows the pattern of the music instead of simply catching the "mood." Nor is music to be used merely as an alternation for or extension of the spoken word. There is a time and place for silence. A congregation trained to pray only to organ accompaniment might have a difficult time transferring this practice to another place. Actions are their own reasons for being. The preparation for the offertory or the time of the Communion can be carried on without musical accompaniment. Organ music stands on its own, has its own purpose, and is never a cover-up for some activity or nonactivity.

The organ has not always provided music for worship. For many centuries all singing was unaccompanied, and the Puritans who lined out the psalms were developing their own form of chant. Unaccompanied music is receiving increasing attention today. Both the texture of the music and the interplay of voices becomes clearer in this form. The choir is a strong voice leading the congregation in song. It was never meant to take away functions from the congregation: to sing " Amens " for them, to make responses in their behalf, or to provide mood music. It was never expected to give a performance. The trend today is to have the choir face one another across a divided chancel or to seat them in a balcony. Their anthem is less often placed in the middle of the service of the Word, where attention would be diverted from the continuity among Scripture, preaching, and prayer. Instead, they may sing a brief Biblical anthem as a gradual linking two lessons. The full anthem is their offering and is sung during the offertory. The choir has a real influence on the kind of music people accept and grow to like; their use of the finest in old and new music broadens the understanding of a congregation.

Worshipers offer to God the best they have or know, and the music (among other factors) is an indication of a congregation's willingness to know and use the finest, or else their easy assumption that whatever they like is the best. The Anglican tradition has put one limitation on choral works: that the words must come from the Bible or the words of the liturgy. This avoids the sentimental and the subjective and ensures that the Biblical word will be heard in as many forms as possible during the service. The final responsibility for what is included in a service lies with the minister. He alone can make sure that choral music is a part of the whole service, moving it from one part to the next, and not a performance that emerges within a service. The organist and/or choir director should be sufficiently knowledgeable in religious music to be able to give trustworthy advice. A visitor to large city churches with paid choirs soon learns how the " concert " approach to music can become obvious in the mood and deportment of a paid choir, which may be not only nonparticipant but even disturbing during parts of a service and come alive only for its own anthem. This is not necessary. To be trained and professional is to be able to fit into whatever setting is necessary. The responsibility lies with those who should be aware of what the choir does for or against the service. When singers are members of a worshiping congregation, they help the others to join the hymns and responses, provide an accompaniment that unifies the service, and become themselves ministers to God with the clergy and others in the congregation. Choirs have been known to help train congregations in singing, either by introducing a new hymn into the service or by taking part in " hymn sings " at some other time.

CHILDREN AND MUSIC

Children often participate in choirs, and this is one of the few ways in which the adult congregation gives them an opportunity to serve. They often show remarkable faithfulness in attending practice and excellent behavior during the service, although this, as well as singing, is part of their training. This can be a primary avenue for educating children in the purposes and meanings of church music.

They can be helped to understand the meaning of worship, the function of their singing in the service, and how to worship. Historically, they continue the long tradition of boys' choirs. Although churches with one children's choir usually make this a mixed one, those with enough children to staff several choirs sometimes find that in the junior age, separate choirs for boys and girls suit the interests of the children, enlist the enthusiasm of the boys, and make possible the use of the special quality of each kind of voice.

Children's choirs can be a part of the total educational experience of the child in the church, but sometimes this work and that of the church school class become competitive. Usually it is a question of time: lack of time or close timing. Churches that take boys' choirs seriously have usually excused the boys from church school on Sunday in order to take part in the warm-up practice of the choir. (Being part of the whole choir is an important aspect of children's choir work.) This removal from the usual church school grouping is no loss if the choir itself can develop a serious program of study and music at the weekday practice. It would necessarily be a group-graded course and might well form a three-year cycle that used the musical materials of worship illustratively in the curriculum. The denominational group-graded curriculum could be the basis, but the skillful teacher would see where hymnody, anthem, and liturgical materials were derived from the material under discussion, whether Biblical or historical.

The problem has more often been psychological: the resistance of the boys who looked upon the release from the church school class, in addition to their inclusion in the adult choir, as a sign that they were too old for religious education. Curriculum materials cannot solve such a problem. Published curriculum, plus teachers, plus setting and general expectations (and requirements) might do so. Often the boys know that their voices are so valued that they can successfully resist any demands except those concerned with singing. There the discipline is absolute, and they accept it because it numbers them with the men.

Music becomes part of religious education for all children from the moment they enter the church school, certainly beginning at the age of three. From that point on, there is one basic criterion for the music used with children: it must be the finest available (to the glory of God and as a " preparation " for the liturgy) and still come within the comprehension of the child. " Comprehension " is not to be taken entirely in an intellectual sense. The arts require an emotional involvement that is apprehension, appreciation, awareness. Intellectual understanding is part, but technical knowledge of a musical composition, although enriching the total understanding, is not sufficient. Child choir members sing difficult music containing words beyond their conceptual comprehension, yet this does not seem to inhibit their ability to sing meaningfully under the choirmaster's direction.

Simplicity is the keynote, requiring a strong melody that is repeated, as in the psalm tunes, with only slight variation. Remembering that even three-year-olds sing Christmas carols with enthusiastic voices, leaders of children need not be timid in introducing music. Complicated rhythms and odd intervals are difficult for children who do not have the intellectual-physical skills to encompass them. The trend in children's hymnody is to put stress on songs of praise and thanksgiving in order to introduce children to the setting for congregational worship. Music from the church hymnal is used whenever possible, even if this is only one line, such as the refrain to " O Come, All Ye Faithful " or to " For the Beauty of the Earth." [27]

Children who attend morning worship need to be helped to understand how to use the hymnal, which is unlike any book with which they have been previously acquainted. It is large and heavy and uses two bars for music. In school, if a songbook is used, only the treble clef with one melody line is provided.[28] Another problem the child faces is that he has been taught to read one line below the next as in paragraph structure. In the hymnal he finds that he must skip three lines (the first line of each succeeding stanza) and move to the next clef. This is confusing until he has been instructed. Obviously, children of primary age are not really equipped to use the hymnal, but to hold the open book is a symbol of participation in the service.

There must be a time when children are taught some of the hymns used by the congregation. In hymn practice they learn the melody by hearing it sung or played so that they can recognize and follow. Although words and music need to be associated from the start, it is also necessary to read the words aloud together so that they make sense and become more than syllables set to music. For this purpose, words may be written on newsprint or chalkboard and placed where all can see, or booklets containing words of hymns may be provided for each child. Here the eye can reinforce the ear. There is no need to memorize (adults do not memorize hymns unless by deliberate reason or through familiarity). More hymns can be practiced and learned. Recordings of choirs singing hymns can be helpful. During hymn practice, the children may join in singing as they hear the record. Records can reinforce learning when used in class as presession background music or an accompaniment to activity work. Piano accompaniment for hymn singing is not necessary and is frequently a hindrance. The instrument takes up room that could be put to better use; it is a constant temptation to children interested either in music or in sound; it is sometimes awkwardly played by willing but unable accompanists, or becomes the vehicle for an elaborate but unhelpful accompaniment. Organ, with its legato tone, is not sharp enough to help children catch the melody. Teachers can be brave and lead the singing with their own voices. A well-tuned xylophone will give that one clear, simple melody line needed. A visitor who is able to play a stringed or wind instrument could make the melodies of hymn tunes sound clearly to a listening group of children.

Practice time is necessary. Although this could be incorporated into a class session at regular intervals — weekly, biweekly, or monthly — there is value in having several classes or grades meet together. This shares the responsibility and makes use of special talents among the teachers. The time becomes more interesting to the children because it is held outside the usual classroom routine. Happy the parish in which children's music becomes the special area of service for someone who wants to help in the church school by offering a specialized skill! Rarely there is a director of children's music who spends time with each age group, starting with rhythms for the three-year-olds. Happy the church whose choir director has an interest in children's music and some knowledge of it, and who will gladly meet with those responsible for children's music and guide their work even though he cannot personally be with the children! Practice sessions are most successful at the kindergarten and primary or lower junior level. Older children are able to follow music. With them it is better to concentrate on knowledge about hymnody. This becomes an enrichment for the regular curriculum, where hymns from the earliest centuries become a way of understanding church history, and hymns using Biblical and theological ideas illustrate and illumine those courses.

A good time to practice music and study about it with children is in a period following their attendance at morning worship. Since such attendance is a growing practice, and the younger children are usually dismissed before the sermon, the succeeding time could well be spent in departmental groups preparing for participation in and enriching of the understanding. Thus the gathering together to learn about hymns and to sing hymns is an important unit in any such program.

MUSIC AND EDUCATION

Liturgical music and religious music are not the same. The former is written specifically to carry the liturgy. The latter is an expression of what the faith means to the composer. Even the use of liturgical materials does not necessarily make liturgical music. Bach's *Mass in B Minor* is an example. Originally written to commend himself to an elector from whom he hoped to obtain an appointment, it is too elaborate to be used as the setting for the Eucharistic service. Liturgical music has to keep moving, illumining the meaning of words and actions. There is no room for repetition of words and elaboration of voices. Sometimes religious music can be incorporated into liturgy; too often, alas, it provides a performance. Each type of music has its place, and people should be acquainted with both for the deepening of their own faith. An important part of the function of a choir is to produce religious music. No one who has ever watched a performance of Benjamin Britten's *Noye's Fludde* doubts that even the littlest child who participates has a renewed understanding of the meaning of creation and redemption. Brahms's *Requiem,* with its thoughtful choice of texts, conveys deeply the meaning of death and resurrection, while Verdi's *Requiem,* using a liturgical text, vividly sounds out the experience of judgment in the magnificent *" Dies Irae "* and the triumph of God's righteousness. Such music finds its place as a special work of the choir performed on Sunday afternoon or evening, or on a special occasion.

Another area of religious music is its popular form. This has been suspect, especially in Protestant circles, where many remember the legacy of revival songs whose sentimental melodies and questionable religious affirmations were decidedly subjective in tone. The erotic element was obvious and too slightly sublimated. Folk music, primarily Negro spirituals and Southern mountain melodies, have a different quality. Honesty and simplicity overcome the naïveté and place spiritual songs in a different order from that of the more contrived gospel songs written by popular religious songwriters (Ira D. Sankey being the most famous) with their deliberate intent to arouse emotions. In religious folk music the Biblical message spoke to a difficult life and the profoundness of the message often comes through, as in "When Israel was in Egypt land: let my people go." There is a sifting process in the preservation of a heritage, and religious music is no exception. A careful examination of the output of the revival era could turn up some good religious songs that should be preserved both as illustrative of the movement and for the permanency of their interpretation of the Christain faith. Today, jazz and contemporary folk music have become forms for popular religious musical expression. Sometimes they are used liturgically: there are settings for the Roman Mass, the Episcopal rite for the Eucharist, the Wesley service. These contemporary forms find popularity especially among student groups. Easy to follow and easy to understand, they find ready acceptance among the young, who are impatient with the forms with which they grew up and feel that this music " speaks " to them. There are also folk and popular settings to traditional or new hymns. As the nineteenth-century gospel songs expressed the emotional needs for love and comfort that the people in isolated pioneer communities felt, so the religious folk songs, sensing the injustice of the society, express the longings and hopes of today's young people. Some of these songs arise from popular folk singers and contain implicit theological comment. Some are deliberate folk settings for known hymn words.[29] (The theology of recurrently " religious " motifs in popular records is more expressive of a sentimental secular religiosity.)

The purpose of religious music is to convey meaning. Words are required to express clearly and with some simplicity the generally accepted meanings of the Christian faith. The feeling-tone of the words should be conveyed by the music. This is a criterion for evaluating hymns and other forms of religious music. New editions of hymnals have occasionally brought well-known hymns startlingly into new focus by changing the tune to which they were set. It is like polishing a piece of silver or moving an object to a new spot in a room where it can really be seen. People are more conscious of music than of words as they sing hymns. The danger is that when music is completely familiar, they will fail to think of the words they sing. It might be helpful to train congregations to accept more than one tune for a hymn in order that they become accustomed to different ways of hearing the meaning expressed.

The person responsible for choosing religious music or hymns needs first to be assured that the words convey the meaning intended. He will then want to know the usefulness of a particular set of words for the place where it is being used in the service. He will next look at the music to see if it enhances the words, if it is a strong tune, and if it is singable.

Although contemporary popular music is having considerable vogue, the church has been slow in accepting contemporary atonal music based often on the twelve-tone scale.[80] Organists are now trained to play music by living composers, so that gathering and departing congregations have become accustomed subliminally to it. Few such tunes have found their way into hymnals. Liturgical settings fare better, especially with the popularity of Healey Willan for the Lutheran and Anglican service music, and contemporary French composers for the Roman rite. Present-day music has affinities with the ancient chants because it relies less on specific accent and is less obviously melodic than classical Western music has been. One hopeful trend in new hymnals lies in the fact that time designations are being omitted — an encouragement to let the melody flow without strong accent.

There are ways of increasing the understanding of a congregation for its musical heritage. Involvement is a primary form of learning. Background material arouses interest. Present-day congregations might be startled to discover that some hymns which they have considered old because of childhood associations are actually new within the historical memory of the Christian community. Such information can be incorporated into the Sunday calendar or whatever occasional informational paper is published, or given orally, either in introducing a hymn, or perhaps more fittingly at the time of announcements. Hymnals usually have an accompanying " Handbook to the Hymnal " which parallels it numerically and gives background information on both words and tunes.[31] No minister can afford to be without this, and it should be available on the bookshelves of every church for the use of all who have responsibilities for teaching.

The education of a congregation is enriched when a basic body of hymns is used and gradually enlarged. People do not avoid the new if there are a reasonable number of familiar hymns remaining to give security. Suppose, however, that one is changing from a gospel songbook to a church hymnal. One could introduce the most solid of the church hymns, so widely used that almost anyone in the congregation will have heard them somewhere. When a new hymn has become familiar, an " old familiar " may be omitted. Any hymn list needs to be under constant supervision if a congregation is to be enabled to accept the new hymns and to have an opportunity to express praise in fresh forms.

Encourage singing as an expression of *worship*. Members of a congregation, if asked why they are singing hymns, would have to pause before answering. " It is announced; it brings the choir in and out; it gives a change of pace or a change of voice." They might even think of the meaning hymns hold for individuals: " Puts one in a mood, expresses aspirations." Primarily, the hymn is meant to be a way by which the whole congregation is involved in the action through which God is worshiped. They join with clergy and choir to praise him around whom the service centers. Hymn-singing has this outward thrust.

A congregation needs opportunities for practicing hymns. Some ministers have provided for this at the time of the announcements and the offering. Since this is not really an " offering," the important meaning of this section of the service becomes unclear. Tunes that are most in need of learning become familiar if used as a prelude, or the first stanza could become a choir introit to which the people listen. A new tune could be used as an offertory anthem. When people have heard a tune once, they are prepared to try to sing it themselves. Opportunities can be provided at other times for the joy of singing together, as at church suppers. Once a year the choir director or choir members might visit a regular meeting of each group, using time there for introducing the purposes of singing in worship, giving background material, and practicing a few unfamiliar hymns. An evening of singing, including music by the choir, would draw people who could become a nucleus for a strong congregational response on Sunday. The Christmas carol evening was mentioned; hymn-singing could also be the focus for structuring a post-Easter, a Lenten, or other Sunday evening event.

Records can familiarize people with new music. A good record player and a growing collection of records will encourage new learning. The resources of the public library are helpful. This is a particularly useful way for becoming acquainted with twentieth-century music. Such records, played quietly, can form a background as people assemble for an afterchurch coffee hour or for various group meetings. Groups can be encouraged to have a program devoted to religious and/or liturgical music, illustrated from records. Young people have begun stimulating discussions on the meaning of worship by listening first to a jazz or folk setting. High school students are sometimes disturbed by this; college students enjoy it.

The vitality of congregational singing has a long tradition in Protestant worship; hymn-singing is increasingly used among Roman Catholics. Congregational singing does not remain vital of itself; it needs the constant stimulus of the introduction of new music, encouragement in singing, introductory material to inform it, and thought concerning the purpose of singing praise.

	COMMUNICATION
CHAPTER 6	THROUGH
	THE LORD'S SUPPER

COMMUNICATION THROUGH THE LORD'S SUPPER

PARTICIPATION IS THE MOST DIRECT FORM of communication. In the Lord's Supper the Christian community has been given an action through which all can participate in worship together. It begins by linking an immediate congregation with groups of Christians who were gathered together in a similar way in the past nearly two thousand years. This brings to mind the Last Supper which Jesus shared with the Twelve and at which he commanded remembrance through its repetition. It is also a reminder of the love that binds the community together: God's love in sending his Son, and the love which he makes possible to those who are committed to him. Maundy Thursday, the yearly remembrance of the Last Supper, takes its name from the words in John's Gospel (ch. 13:34-35) : " A new commandment [*mandatum*] I give to you, that you love one another; even as I have loved you, that you also love one another. By this all men will know that you are my disciples, if you have love for one another."

One recalls other occasions on which Jesus blessed and broke and gave the bread: to the multitude, to the couple whom he met on the road to Emmaus on the resurrection evening, to the disciples who were met by their risen Lord as they returned to shore from a fishing trip on the Lake of

Galilee. They always recognized him in the breaking of the bread. He was among them, giving it to them, completing their fellowship in him. One remembers also the reiteration of the tradition by the apostle Paul in I Cor. 11:23-26, the earliest written account. The apostle ends the description with his own words, " For as often as you eat this bread and drink the cup, you proclaim the Lord's death until he comes." This is reminiscent of Jesus' words, " Truly, I say to you, I shall not drink again of the fruit of the vine until that day when I drink it new in the kingdom of God" (Mark 14:25). Participation in the Supper, in addition to linking the present company with a past fellowship, also links them with a future fellowship and sets the thoughts of the present Christian community on the fact that there is before them the time of fulfillment, known only to God, which will be the consummation of his purposes for mankind. One could simply tell all these things to a congregation, of course, yet it would not have nearly the immediate meaning that it does if they actually take part in the event in their own situation, and do so repeatedly.

The Lord's Supper teaches because it is a dramatic action. It is not simply descriptive. Some Christian groups have stripped it to this retelling and have confined their participation in this form of worship simply to having someone read the account in I Corinthians, followed, perhaps, by a brief prayer and the distribution of the elements. This is certainly better than ignoring the Supper, especially when this form is repeated frequently as an understanding that this seems to have been the practice of the primitive church. Since, however, the Lord's Supper is a reenactment of an event, it is faithfully reenacted only through action. The leader must take the bread and openly, before the people, break it. He must take the cup and raise it up as one would for a toast or for a blessing (as the head of the Jewish household does today in the blessing of the cup before the Sabbath meal and during the Pass-over meal.)

Traditional American Protestant hesitancy to act here reflects a background of intellectualism, anti-Catholicism, the fear of suggesting magic, and just plain awkwardness in the face of the dramatic. Dramatic action in Anglo-Saxon Protestantism has largely been confined to the pul-pit. When the preacher was dramatic in voice, gesture, and appearance, the people could respond emotionally to him and thus satisfy a deep-felt need. The meaning is clear in the reactions to a sermon: "That fed me; that was most satisfying." So the emotional response to the Sacrament of the Word (in Karl Barth's phrase) has usually replaced rather than supplemented or led up to the emotional re-sponse of the Sacrament of the Table. The minister rather than the Word could (and sometimes did) become the emotional focus of the congregation.

If the minister is to act, so too should the people. It is not enough that they sit in their places to receive what is brought to them. Is that the way one acts at a meal? One goes to the table. The assumption of the Reformed Church of France (made evident in the interiors of some of the newest churches in other countries) is that people will surround the table. Since no area would be large enough for most congregations, they come in groups. Some archi-tects have planned for an extension table which, at the time of the Lord's Supper, is opened wide as a part of the preparation for the event. How people receive the bread and cup, whether standing, seated, or kneeling, seems to be part of individual tradition but is also connected with the degree to which this is looked upon as a communal action or a personal one. Each human action reflects meaning, so that even the manner of participation in the Lord's Supper is expressing meaning at the same time that it con-veys meaning. There is a distinct difference in connotation between " receiving " the bread and " taking " the bread.

The first suggests acceptance and receptiveness on the part of the worshiper to whom God is giving this bread; the second stresses the initiative of the worshiper who " takes " that which is offered. It is simply a matter of whether the stress is on the divine action or on the human response. Each is a way of understanding the act and thus of inwardly learning the act.

Action demands the active participation of all present. They need to use varied motions; they need to speak, sing, and pray in unison. This interaction between the presiding minister and the congregation provides a liturgy of thanksgiving in which communal participation makes it memorable, and makes possible the continuous repetition without monotony.

Communication through the Lord's Supper brings into focus many aspects of the Biblical understanding of God's relationship to man. It suggests the whole idea of sacrifice (" This is my body which is given for you "), which has its place in the Old Testament. There are many kinds of sacrifice, basically delineated in the Priestly writings in later Exodus, Leviticus, and Deuteronomy: sin offerings, peace offerings, thank offerings. Some offerings were burned completely to the glory of God, and other sacrifices were divided among the priests. There were meal (grain) offerings and animal offerings. These actively expressed through visible form the people's acknowledgment that all things came from God and that they owed to him the first fruits of all they possessed. Redemption was also involved, for there lingered the memory of tribes in some distant past that had sacrificed even the firstborn child, whereas the Hebrew people redeemed their children by the gift of animal sacrifice. Sacrifice was not looked upon as deprivation — a modern misuse of the term. Sacrifice was a joyous act of giving, not withdrawing but outgoing. Modern men forget that among some tribal groups a person chosen as a sacrifice to a deity was highly honored. His preparation was accomplished with ceremony; he became himself a symbol of the holy, since he was dedicated to the god; the " dread " connected with the giving up of life was mixed as much with awe as with fear, for no one expected a long life and he could hardly die more gloriously. Christians might well look upon Jesus' sense of sacrificing his life in this way, for he belonged to the ancient world and would have known a positive rather than a negative view of sacrifice.

The Lord's Supper brings to mind other meals described in the New Testament in addition to those earlier mentioned as having possible Eucharistic significance, times when Jesus was known among people by his presence at their table: Zacchaeus, Mary and Martha, Peter, Levi the Pharisee. One is reminded of the three accounts of the Last Supper in the Gospel narratives, and in the differing approach of the Fourth Gospel. John's Gospel places the pronouncements on " I am the bread of life " (ch. 6:35) just after one narrative of the feeding of the multitude, and surrounds the upper room narrative with the washing of the disciples' feet and four chapters (chs. 13 to 17) of discourse ending with the prayer for the disciples. These narratives point to the experience of the Lord's dwelling among his people, intimately sharing with them occasions of human fellowship which show warmth, assurance, and mutual affection. Meditating on these events, one might well be led to transfer this same presence to the reenactment of the meal in its symbolic form within the setting of Christian worship.

The Acts of the Apostles also mentions the breaking of bread at several points, as earlier noted. This was a mark of the first days of the Jerusalem group after the experience of Pentecost. Paul met with the congregation at Ephesus one night for the breaking of bread; he participated in this with the elders of the church at Melita; he broke bread for the storm-tossed and terrified gathering on a ship at sea. The passage in I Corinthians from which the authoritative description of the Supper is frequently quoted is set in the framework of his discussion of the practices of that congregation (not quite as they should have been), and the apostle's warning has had the unfortunate effect of causing some Christian groups to stress the possibility of condemnation through improper participation in the Lord's Supper instead of rejoicing in the gift of the presence of the Lord among his people. This threatening aspect has given an opening for hedging the Supper around with requirements for sanctity or sinlessness at the moment, for various forms of confession, valid Baptism, confirmation and clergy orders, and for the exclusion of all but members of the particular group who can be trusted to keep the prerequisites. Eventually, the ecclesiastical body feels itself responsible for guarding the purity of the Lord's Table. What is to be the basis for admission: Baptism, an act of commitment, membership in a particular branch of the church, auricular confession, attendance at a preparatory service? The question has as many answers as there are guardian ecclesiastical groups.

The Supper focuses attention on the Biblical understanding of eschatology, a subject seldom under discussion in today's world except in the upper intellectual reaches of Christendom and in the preaching of sectarian groups. Eschatology is plainly present in the accounts of the Last Supper: it is a foretaste of the future. The source of its joy is this: drinking the cup *new*. Beyond the pain of the present lies the future when the reign of God will be made clear to a redeemed creation. The forward look is as important an element as is the backward look. The memory of how God has acted to save his people is the assurance that gives hope for his future saving action. In times of stress the people of God are most comforted by participation in the Lord's Supper. They can indeed give thanks, for he has not left them comfortless or without hope.

Promise for the future is assured because of fulfillment in the past and in the present.

There are four actions in the Biblical account and these have always been a part of its repetition: the offering of the bread and wine — these symbols of daily food — the consecration in thanksgiving that God may use them, the breaking of the bread as a reminder of Christ's body broken for us, and the distribution to all who worship that they may participate anew in his life.[32]

MEANINGS IN THE LORD'S SUPPER

The very term " the Lord's Supper " suggests the parallel of a meal. This particular meal may or may not have been part of the Passover Seder itself; in the early church it may or may not have had some connection with a fellowship meal called the Love Feast. Christians today are familiar with the parish fellowship meal as well as with meals which small groups hold, and they are familiar with the Lord's Supper as the symbolic meal.

Think for a moment of what a meal connotes. It is one time of day when the family try to be together. Food itself, through psychological-physiological mechanisms, is comforting and makes it possible for people to be at ease and to enjoy one another (unless parents are upset over children's infraction of behavior rules) . The remembrance of family meals is a part of everyone's past. Special meals — at Christmas, Thanksgiving, birthdays, or weddings — are times for joyous celebration. Such an event often includes the wider family: grandparents, aunts, uncles, cousins. Children's birthdays are celebrated with friends. Privacy becomes broadened to include others; the intimacy of the family group is enlarged to include the larger family and friends — even sometimes the stranger who has nowhere else to go on a holiday. The emotional intensity of fellowship on such occasions runs deep. Eating may be enjoyable, but long after the menu has been forgotten, one recalls the feelings that accompanied the occasion.

Meals also have connotations of providing and giving. There is an outgoing direction, away from the self, which includes love and generosity, concern for the other. Somebody prepares this food. This is hard work, time-consuming, but the pleasure lies in the anticipation of the joy of the fellowship in which one has had such a necessary part. The guests who may offer to help know that whatever they do is only a symbolic token, for the privilege of giving this meal is reserved for those who have prepared it and invited others to share in the feast. To serve is a ceremonial honor; both host and hostess know their parts, and at the family meal both mother and father have particular roles. They indicate the manner of serving and where each person shall sit. (Does anyone ever approach a table without remembering the parable of the man who seated himself near the head only to be told to go lower?)

Receiving is the appropriate response of the guests. This is neither easy nor natural for all people. Some feel that they must always come bearing a gift — not crassly in the form of payment, not exactly in the form of an offering, but perhaps just to provide some sort of equivalent. Some are careful to extend a return invitation — and soon — perhaps because of sheer generosity and enjoyment of the opportunity to entertain, perhaps to return the courtesy and even the score (again, not in any crude way). But those who can openly and joyfully receive are "paying" simply by their presence and their enjoyment. This is the gift they bring; this is the gift which host and hostess receive, if their entertaining has been to this purpose and not as a part of the merry-go-round of fulfilling social obligations. Receiving is so basic a factor in the religious understanding of Christianity — relationship to God and to the community — that it is important to look at how it works out in this one facet of ordinary human existence.

Giving and receiving are reciprocal actions. The one who prepares the meal offers (gives) it, and the guests receive that which they have not done for themselves. At the same time, the guest offers his company, his enjoyment, his participation, and this the host receives as something he could not have by himself.

Here is a prototype of the relationship between Christ and his people. He is at the Table, among his people, giving to them as he gave to the first disciples, or to the disciples at Emmaus. Here is a particular way of knowing that the living Lord comes to his own. To be sure, he is with them always, in all times and all places, but there is power in the localizing of his presence in this place, in this moment, which in no way could suggest that God is not everywhere in his world. This kind of event left the disciples at Emmaus remarking, " Did not our hearts burn within us? " and left the disciples at Pentecost saying that the Spirit had descended like flames of fire. Countless Christians have had this feeling as they participated in the Lord's Supper. When this sense of his presence illumines the meal, there is indeed joy and thanksgiving. There is no question of dulling the experience by repetition. Do people stop eating together? or having friends come to dinner? Love and joy are deepened and increased by the constant repetition of mutual presence.

Congregations, assembled for this meal in the assurance that God comes offering and serving, find themselves in the position of receiving and accepting. Westerners would much rather be the initiators, active, doing. They are uncomfortable in having another do something for them. To have a superior serve makes them uncomfortable, almost to the point of pain. Only by domesticating God to the American Dad can his worshipers accept from Him, and then they take the position of small children to whom such care is owed. The Christian assembly is not meant to be like that. Christ is the Head of his disciples, who are to be as apostles, called and sent. To receive from him requires a particular attitude which is more passive than active, self-effacing rather than self-asserting. The personal action lies in having come, participating in praise and thanksgiving. One has already offered himself: his life and his money, which symbolize life through work. But in the climax of the Eucharistic banquet, the worshiper receives. Receptivity, surrender, is the action. The joy lies in the depths of this communion with him who is both holy and loving.

Symbols of creation and of redemption are to be found here. The elements are a part of God's creation, of the world which he made and called good, of the earth which he created and made to bear food for the sustaining of life. (This also comes to mind when one thinks of the thanksgiving before a family meal.) These same symbols take on the meanings of redemption, of the sacrifice made, of the life given in behalf of another. Here is death and resurrection, the Supper before Calvary and the meal after Easter. As Baptism is the once-and-for-all participation with Christ in his death and resurrection, here is the repeatable participation in his death (" my body," " my blood ") and resurrection (" in remembrance," " until . . . I drink it new "). This should not be too difficult to understand psychologically, since all beings come to birth through feeding on the blood of the mother, and the most primitive tribes have had ceremonies by which they symbolically partook of the life of another and greater in order to participate in his life and particularly in his courage.

Creation and redemption evoke feelings of joy, wonder, and awe. These become part of the response, the " mood " of the Eucharist. There is the adoration felt in the presence of the Holy One. There is thanksgiving for what God has done and is doing for his people and in his world. There is joy, for this is the concomitant of love; and love is the response of the worshiper in the presence of the Lord, who seeks and saves, who sustains and heals.

Why have so many Protestant groups seemingly avoided

an experience that can be described in such glowing terms? The Catholic traditions, Eastern and Roman, have continued the Eucharist as the central action of the weekly assembly, although it must be admitted that dwindling numbers have availed themselves of full participation. Doubtless historical memory is involved in the Protestant attitude. The Middle Ages had seen the Supper surrounded by so many *caveats* that the faithful deemed it safer to avoid contact except when necessary; hence the eventual requirement for annual reception of the Sacrament. Some Protestant groups have taken the warning to the Corinthians with great seriousness and asked if it might not easily apply to them. Better to partake sparingly than to run the risk of condemnation! Still other groups have interpreted the Lord's Supper as a form of the proclamation of the gospel, parallel to preaching. This viewpoint was espoused by Zwingli early in the Reformation and adhered to by the Reformed Church in Switzerland. A view common within American Protestant groups understands the Lord's Supper as a memorial meal, a solemn recollection of the death of the Lord. The observance becomes simplified, the mood somber. This seems to be the viewpoint of some groups which observe the Supper as part of the weekly service: Disciples of Christ, Mormons, Plymouth Brethren. Practical considerations have entered into some decisions as to the frequency of observance. When the Methodists were serving an ever-expanding frontier in the nineteenth century, an ordained minister could not possibly reach each congregation frequently; hence the quarterly conference (or congregational meeting) which included the observance of the Holy Communion. Another viewpoint has affirmed that frequent Communion would "take the edge off it," make it less impressive, make it seem routine. This could happen to any form of service, including the preaching service. It is less apt to happen if there is a sense of vital expectancy, the assurance that this is the time and place when Christ is present among his people, when the people actively respond to him and to one another. The theological understanding of the Lord's Supper is an important factor.

In *The Celebration of the Gospel*,[33] five aspects of the Lord's Supper are listed, and the list is suggestive: *proclamation* of the good news; *witness* to what God has done and is doing to save his people; *the double offering* — man offers himself and his possession, God offers himself and his redemption; *participation*-communion, the presence of the Lord; *thanksgiving*-Eucharist, the foretaste of the Kingdom.

Unfortunately, some Protestant groups have been taught to regard the Lord's Supper as the solemn remembrance of a death, resulting in the awkward, uncomfortable feelings with which modern Americans often approach the fact of death. Understandably, they are relieved to have it occur seldom. At the same time, the very fact of infrequency makes it seem odd and increases the discomfort. Only the frequent participation in an act makes it familiarly acceptable. Some avoid even this infrequent observance. At the opposite pole is an attitude that speaks of " celebrating " the Eucharist. These words suggest joy, gladness, approachability, and warmth. A celebration includes everyone. How sad is an attempted celebration which few people attend! Numbers at a celebration heighten the feeling of proclamation and witness. It is an unfortunate misunderstanding of the purpose of this celebration if some stay but do not receive the elements, or if some leave before the Eucharistic service begins. Who, invited to a home, would excuse himself and leave before the meal was served except under extraordinary and previously explained reasons?

EDUCATION AND THE LORD'S SUPPER

Learning by doing is assumed to be a prime way of reinforcing learning. One can learn all *about* the Lord's

Supper as an intellectual exercise, taking the learner into sociology, psychology, theology, philosophy, history, and literature, but this will never give fullness of meaning. The outside observer is a valuable source for the understanding of the ceremonial life (the cultus) of any religious group, but his stance and therefore his observations and learnings are of a different order from those of the involved participant. The member of the Christian community is surely not an outside observer; thus he can never understand the Lord's Supper simply by learning about it. In the middle of the fourth century, when Christianity had become an acceptable form of religion in the Roman world and converts were crowding the churches for baptismal instruction, this instruction was carefully planned. In the weeks of preparation they were taught the Creed (the faith of the church), the Ten Commandments (the rule of the church), and the Lord's Prayer (the prayer of the church). These were memorized and explained in lecture form, phrase by phrase. Baptism was held on Easter Eve and the new Christians participated with the congregation in the Easter celebration of the Lord's Supper. In the succeeding week they returned for further lectures, in which the meaning of these two significant rites was explained more fully *after* their participation. These early educators recognized that only after people have experienced are they able to look at the experience and to begin to understand. Moreover, this suggests that an understanding of such significant rites cannot be accomplished all at once, but is unfolded throughout life. Christians have usually increased in their understanding of the Communion by participation in it, and have found it an avenue for deepening their awareness of God's presence and strengthening their assurance that his Spirit guided them in their work. One thanksgiving prayer ends: " Assist us with thy grace, that we may continue in that holy fellowship, and do all such good works as thou hast prepared for us to walk in." [34] This participation is, moreover, an appropriation of what God offers, and not a work by which one can prove himself to God. Participation is involvement.

If one is to learn by doing, the question immediately arises about who shall be permitted to participate. The Orthodox Church baptizes infants, confirms them with the laying on of hands, and immediately gives them the Communion. The Roman Catholic Church baptizes infants, admits them to Communion at the age of six or seven, when the ability to reason makes deliberate sin an actuality and the Sacrament promises the grace of God for strengthening. Protestant groups, whether baptizing in infancy or at an " age of discretion " have always made admission to the Communion dependent upon the personal act of commitment, whether this be adult Baptism, confirmation, or " joining the church " — in other words " full membership." How, then, are the young, or even adults who have not yet made a commitment of faith, to be introduced to the meaning of the rite?

One method has been the " model " Communion service, sometimes suggested in a curriculum guide for the junior age. In this, a group of elders or deacons come to the class and enact the Communion service. The purpose is to show this to the children in a relaxed and familiar atmosphere during their regular class time, where they will also have the freedom to ask questions and to be given explanation. This fails at the point of being a dramatization; it is not quite real, and the children know it. This is a way to help them understand intellectually the words and actions. It could, however, simply make the whole rite seem odd and strange, for when separated from the feelings and total surrounding action, the bare facts and action do not make sense, certainly not to an American sixth-grade child.

Another method has been that of the " explained service." Here the table is set in any room of the church; a classroom or a living room setting. The minister conducts it; those present who are eligible receive the elements. During the celebration there are pauses at which a narrator, standing to one side, explains the meaning of what is happening. This should be done by a teacher, or an elder or deacon. The explanation needs to be simple, unobtrusive, and brief. It still may become an interruption instead of really fitting into the parts of the service. This is the drawback. The real is constantly being interrupted. But it is a step better than the " model " method because the intellectual explanation is combined with (even if intruded into) the totality of the full experience. Particularly important is the fact that all can sense the response of those who are participating in terms of receiving the elements. This cannot be explained, nor should it be, but it is an important part of the learning experience for the children.

A third method is to have a picture book that describes the service for children. Here the simple words on one page will explain the action depicted on the facing page. The Roman Catholic Church has published several such books, for children as well as for adults. The best ones, done for youth and adults, by using excellent photographs convey to some extent the mood as well as the meaning.[35] The book can be a useful tool in conjunction with some form of participation in the service itself. Children and unbaptized adults who have attended the Communion service and sensed some of its meaning are able to carry this memory into the class group, where the pictures and the text of the book recall the actual event and provide the means for discussing the meaning of what is happening.

The catechumen (for this was the ancient name for the learner) could be encouraged to attend the Eucharistic service, participating in everything but the actual reception of the elements. This makes him familiar with the service, and gives him time to become familiar with all the surrounding action, including the responses of the congregation. Such partial participation, involving the deliberate withholding of full participation, can have a positive value, for it engenders anticipation: " When you are old enough, when you are prepared, when you feel ready to make your profession of faith and commitment." There are some who believe that children thus deprived feel left out, that nothing should be offered adults that is not offered them. Where has it ever been true that children were expected to have everything adults have, simply because they happened to be in the same place at the same time? The inclusion of children in the service is sufficient. Their joy and sense of importance comes from being in the " big " church or in the "adult " service from their earliest years, just as they find joy in being included in family celebrations, though they may fall asleep in a strange bed long before the evening is over.

Remaining away from full participation until some generally acceptable point (which may or may not be some ultimate form of profession) is a part of the education in the meaning of the event. The Eucharist assumes importance if it is precious to those who hold the key to admission. They must have good reasons, and one does well to prepare himself, for then he can accept a full place in the community with a sense of solemn, joyous commitment. This is true whether for a child of seven, a youth of eighteen, or a fully grown adult. The early church excluded the catechumens after the reading and hearing of the Word, the instructional service. No one unbaptized could even watch the celebration. To participate in the Christian rite was illegal and therefore dangerous. No one dared risk giving the knowledge of his own involvement into the hands of another who was not fully committed to live or die for Christ. Today life is easier for most Christian communities; the partially committed are invited to stay for the whole service in the hope that this will elicit from them finally a full commitment of life.

There is need for more teaching about the Eucharist to accompany the celebration. This could sometimes come through preaching, as the pericopes suggest the theme: the feeding of the multitude, manna in the wilderness, the supper at Emmaus, the institution of the Supper, and so on. Such opportunities could be used to the benefit of any congregation, for the ignorance of the people is not only surprising but disturbing. They know how they should interpret and how they should feel — but the actuality does not match the theory. The minister has an important responsibility here.

The ever-useful Sunday bulletin and other printed media immediately suggest themselves because they seem to be read by congregations. A brief paragraph on the subject might carry weight. For those who read, a whole literature is growing up in scholarly yet readable books — one thinks especially of the Ecumenical Studies in Worship series.[36] These can also be used in study groups. New curriculum materials are including units on worship, usually planned for boys and girls from third grade through high school, less frequently for adults. A prayer group could surely enter into the subject of the meaning of the Communion. Meditation on the Eucharistic prayers, the Sanctus, the thanksgiving, the words with which the elements are received, the closing, can lead to deep and lasting enrichment of their life of devotion, individually and corporately.

The house church Communion has recently been popularized through experiences in England.[37] Here is an opportunity for the actual participation of a small group in the familiar setting of a neighbor's dining room or kitchen through which church members can become more deeply related to one another through their meeting with Christ. After the service, opportunity is given for exploration of what this has meant, what it could mean, and why it is central in Christian worship.

These are just suggestions. The present fashioners of the revival of worship in all branches of Christendom hope that a lively interest in the centrality of this Sacrament will continue to grow. As this comes about, there will be increasing need and opportunity for various avenues by which this corporate action of devotion may be strengthened and made more understandable to the deepening of individual commitment and the witness of the whole church. The peace of God is invoked upon a people being sent out into a turbulent world. They need all the strength available from sharing in this heavenly feast.

CHAPTER 7

THE VARIED SIGNS FOR WORSHIP

CONGREGATIONAL WORSHIP does not happen in a vacuum. Signs surround the action to explain and to enhance. The arrangement of materials and the progression of the action itself signify the purpose and the unity of the whole. The choice of the spoken or the sung word, and the places were there is silence also have significance for the direction of worship.

The whole body is part of the action of worship. Particular reasons dictate when a congregation rises, sits, or kneels. Such habits become so associated with specific actions that a person confronted with a different set of responses in a similar situation feels uncomfortable. A congregation usually stands to sing, but occasionally a prayer response is sung seated or kneeling. A congregation usually sits to listen, but in several traditions stands to hear the Scripture. In some traditions people stand to pray; in others, they sit or kneel. Other actions have had symbolic denotation: the sign of the cross made on the forehead of a person at Baptism, in blessing over the people by the clergyman, or by individuals at certain points in the service to remind themselves that they belong to Christ. Motion is employed by the clergyman as he goes from one part of the sanctuary to another: from lectern to pulpit to altar, to the chancel steps or to a litany desk in the midst of the people. The motions he uses in the dedication of the people's offerings are symbolic. The actions enjoined upon him in the celebration of the Eucharist are highly symbolic, whether elaborate or simple.

Everyday elements used in worship point to the material quality of Christianity. All in God's creation is good, and matter need not be spiritualized. Water is used in Baptism (and the practice of dipping the fingers in " holy water " — that is, water that has been blessed — to make the sign of the cross is a reminder of Baptism). Bread and wine (or its equivalent), used for the Communion, are life-sustaining materials. Some traditions have used such Old Testament customs as oil for anointing, and incense to symbolize prayer lifted to heaven. Salt placed on the tongue at Baptism is a reminder that the Christian is to be as salt that has not lost its savor. Such a use of the tangible emphasizes the fact that in every action the whole person is involved. It becomes an object lesson. It adds the senses of touch and smell to the experiences of hearing and speaking and the varied actions involving seeing. Worship that fails to use the kinetic senses is to that extent impoverished. There are always some Christian groups which consider these customs elaborations or distractions. To them the Word simply heard and perhaps sung will be understandable. While this may seem to be an intellectualistic approach, it has appealed not only to the educated but frequently to low-income groups, whose meeting places and services may reflect the simplicity, even the barrenness and drabness, of everyday existence and the general neighborhood. Others have held that people who cannot be reached intellectually can become aware emotionally, and that even intellectual learning is reinforced by auxiliary means. They look on light, color, sound, fragrance, touch, as expressing the glory of God and the joy of celebration. Criticism has been made that people can be reached and even swayed by their emotions on a shallow level without really understanding, or that the glamorous can be used to mislead or to appeal only to the emotions. An understanding of the reasons (cultural as well as religious) for each type of tradition helps one to understand them all, wherever individual preferences may lie. The problem comes when a group absolutizes its customs, for this would suggest that openness to others and the possibility of change — either toward simplicity or ornamentation — is a threat.

Whatever the intention, the eyes see; and what they see is a sign of the meaning of worship in a particular meeting place. Hagia Sophia, the greatest church in Christendom, was built under the Emperor Justinian in the sixth century to the glory of God and the prestige of Justinian. Admitting this fact, it is nevertheless a wonder of man's artistry and of his use of God's gifts. This is acknowledged by the Government of Turkey, which no longer uses it as a mosque but is restoring its original mosaics and preserving it as a museum representative of the preceding culture. The cathedrals of Europe arose in the late Middle Ages. Although they doubtless served a sociological purpose in keeping thousands of monks at work (so why hurry in the building?), they were also expressions of the devotion of people whose artistic gifts were poured out in religious response at a time when the secular had not yet come into the foreground. The New England meetinghouse, with its gradual development into the Georgian colonial style, provides another example of the fusion of the sociological and the religious. When people become wealthier and aesthetically more sophisticated, they reflect this in their public buildings as well as in their private homes.

Such factors still enter into the building of a church. Sometimes there is less distinction between traditions than there is among examples of any particular tradition. The arrangement of the interior of the church is supposed to represent definite theological understandings of worship and of man's approach to God. The most obvious factor is that of the central focus for the worshiper. The Reformed tradition has had the pulpit, large, well- proportioned, and high, the principal center for attention. This emphasized to all who sat beneath it that the hearing of the Word in Scripture and the preaching of the Word were the most important elements in the service of worship. The Communion table, set at ground level in front of the people, suggested the simplicity and intimacy of the Supper.

The Catholic tradition has put the table high, central, and far away, with the pulpit closer to the people, emphasizing the intimacy of the homily and the awesome approach to the altar, to which the people go up. Today there is a shifting in location of these two essential pieces of furniture. Continental Reformed churches have made an impressive effect by putting table and pulpit in proximity. Others place the pulpit back of and slightly above the table. Prominence is given to the latter both by its place in the center of the chancel and by its great size, which the people may surround, thus symbolizing the inextricability of the two symbols. The Catholic tradition, like the Lutheran and Anglican traditions, is cutting the altar from the wall, where it has been since the Gothic period, and returning it to the center of the chancel, where it was in the earliest centuries. The minister as president is seated behind the table; the people surround it. The lectern is disappearing, its functions being absorbed into those of the pulpit, emphasizing the fact that the preached Word proceeds from the Word in Scripture. The Bible itself is a symbol: where it is placed and how it is used have meaning.

As the furniture is symbolic, so also are the smaller objects, which traditionally have been cross, candles, and flowers. When the table was far in the back, these could without danger or difficulty be placed on or near it. Clearly, the churches which placed all these objects on the Communion table itself were rarely going to use it for its originally intended purpose. Other churches used a retable in back. Now that the table is to stand forth austerely and to be used more often, what of the objects? The cross is being suspended from wall or ceiling. It might be an uncomfortably large wooden cross and even have upon it the figure of the Crucified. There is something rather too " neat " about a shining brass cross or an elaborately jeweled one. When viewing a large and simple cross, the mind's eye supplies the figure. There can be symbols within symbols, and the purpose of this or any other symbol is to evoke meaning and response in the viewer.

Two candles are required for the Eucharistic service in the Catholic and Anglican traditions. In contemporary buildings these are frequently placed in tall, free-standing holders or set on the table in squat glass or metal candlesticks, unobtrusively out of the way of the action, yet burning clearly and steadily as reminders that Christ is the Light of the World. (Meanings tend to accumulate around symbols after an original purpose has been forgotten. The purpose of putting candles on a table has always been to give light for those who eat. The symbolic meaning grows up later, at least in part for teaching purposes.)

Flowers are festive signs. Their manner of use in a particular church tends to indicate the cultural practices of the people. The tendency is toward placing them in background niches when they are being used. Imitation flowers are never worthy of being used in the worship of the true God. There could be a temptation: plastic flowers look so real and are so easy to take care of! The use of flowers can serve the purpose of enhancing the mood and appearance of the chancel area, reminding the congregation of creation and of resurrection. Flowers become an offering for those who provide them. They are given to the glory of God and frequently in memory of members of the Christian community who have died and now live with him. Thus the church militant and the church triumphant are linked, and the faith of the one in the other kept fresh. The flowers also symbolize the concern of the congregation for its people, since most churches distribute them after the service to members who are in joy, pain, or sorrow.

Windows can be an aid to worship and a source for teaching. The elaborate stained glass of the Middle Ages told the Biblical stories to the unlettered. Intense concentration is required to identify the stories, and the modern pilgrim usually is grateful for a guide. More obvious in design and less valued are the nineteenth-century American picture windows (including those from Tiffany and LaFarge) which depict the stories clearly, though in more sentimental terms. The colored glass found in country churches will frequently contain symbols that are reminders of favorite Biblical passages: the lily, the sheaf of wheat, the anchor of hope. Today, abstract art is being used where stained glass lends itself to such form. The deep reds and blues that marked the Connick medieval-type windows earlier in the century have been enhanced by the use of green, violet, orange. The sharpness of modern life shines through these windows. They teach by mood rather than through specific pictures, seeking to express the meanings conveyed by the church and its worship.

Next to the table, the central symbol of the church is the baptismal font, since this signifies the rite of initiation into the Christian fellowship. The size of the font reflects the practice of baptism by immersion or pouring/sprinkling. The baptistry in a Baptist church usually has been in the center rear of the chancel, although some new churches are building it to the side of the church, suggesting that the place for the once-for-all Sacrament is not the same as that of the oft-repeated one. Ancient churches had a separate baptistry, and some of these (as at Ravenna) are among the best-preserved of ancient Christian buildings.[38] When the baptistry was moved inside the church, it was usually set apart, either beside the entrance of the church or to one side at the rear. This was to symbolize the fact that Baptism was the mode of entrance upon the Christian life. The newly baptized could walk down the center aisle to join the baptized at the joyful feast. Today in American Protestant congregations it is frequently the custom to incorporate Baptism into a Sunday morning service as a reminder that the whole people of God are involved in the nurture of new Christians. Thus the font has been moved to the front and side of the nave, as the entrance to the chancel.

In early centuries Baptism was administered on Easter Eve, in connection with several other rites, including the lighting of a tall candle — the paschal candle — which was used at each service during the forty days of the Easter season. This is a baptismal candle, symbolizing the new life in Christ which comes through Baptism and through Easter. The use of a special candle at Baptism is common to Orthodox, Catholic, and Anglican traditions as new life is lighted in Christ.

The shape of the church itself carries symbolic meaning. The long narrow reaches of a Gothic cathedral impress the visitor with the awesomeness of God, whom one apprehends from afar. The rectangular New England meetinghouse, and most subsequent Protestant architecture, was planned for a congregation to sit in rows, with attention focused on hearing the pastor. Contemporary churches are designed in varying forms. The fish, so-called, is an elliptical shape which has length and yet curves to bring the people together. Primarily, this tries to say that the church is a nave, a ship, Noah's ark, the whale, and *ichthys* (fish), the Greek letters that spell out an acrostic for "Jesus Christ, Son of God, Savior." The congregation are seated on three sides, the choir and clergy form the fourth side, all drawn into a joint action. Such a church is not intended for seeing and hearing one person but for seeing and participating in actions and words. Thus the building conveys an understanding of worship.

The position of the choir is an indication of its role as well as that of the congregation. A choir high and lifted up at the center front of the congregation suggests not so much assisting the congregation as performing for it. Even the choir placed on either side of a divided chancel can be performers. This particular practice comes from the monastic churches in England, where the monks who sang the daily offices sat in the long choir, with its altar at the head, and the people gathered in the nave, separated from them by a door, having in their sight the " people's altar." This makes a distinct separation of choir and people, while giving a place of visual prominence to the choir. The old New England churches, like the Catholic tradition, placed the choir in a balcony, set apart but where their voices float down upon the congregation, and where the choir can look directly upon the action in the chancel. The trend in contemporary architecture of putting the Communion table in front center, with the congregation surrounding it, suggests that the placement of the choir needs rethinking.

Symbols include the classical sign symbols that one finds frequently used in churches. Some of these are ancient and often quite unintelligible to the modern congregation. A symbol is a word picture that can evoke an emotional response as well as an intellectual one. The cross does this. Even the young child can apprehend some meaning when he is told: " The cross tells of Jesus' death and that on Easter Day, God raised him from the dead, so that he is always with us. It reminds us of God's love." The cross has other meanings which elicit both intellectual and emotional response: sacrifice, salvation, and redemption. Words like these are tied in with secular meanings which may obscure as often as they illumine. The symbol provides a scope for breadth and depth of interpretation that no simply descriptive word can supply.

The eagle at the lectern is a reminder of Isaiah's " They shall mount up with wings like eagles "; the Alpha and Omega convey the idea that God is the beginning and the end, while the triangle suggests the Trinitarian understanding of God. The Chi Rho monogram is made from the first two letters of the Greek word for Christ, and the IHS symbol uses the three letters of the abbreviation for the Greek word for Jesus: iota, eta, and sigma. The vine suggests the Biblical " I am the vine, you are the branches." Each of the four Evangelists has his own symbol. And so it goes! The modern mind seems less attuned to liturgical symbols in spite of the fact that all artistic forms today are highly symbolic, and frequently also abstract: poetry, drama, sculpture, painting, the dance, and music. Letters are symbols which each culture arranges into words with particular meanings. Numbers are another set of symbols. Mathematics today is highly symbolic. The symbol is an economic form of expression. What a mathematician says by means of signs and symbols on one page would take many pages of words to explain. So, too, are the symbols used in churches. But if the symbols have lost their meaning, it is futile to use them simply for decoration. There might be no alternative but to omit them. On the other hand, they may simply have been neglected by a rationalistic generation that had no use for them, and need only to be explained anew to a generation that might thereafter find satisfaction through such sharp, brief speech. Some new symbols have been developed, but they do not seem to have any great power to lay hold of the imagination. When one is looking for new symbols, it should be remembered that the strength of the old symbols has been that they pointed to God and his activity. They were reminders of the good news and gave assurance of redemption.

SIGNS OF THE SEASONS

In addition to signs for worship that can be seen, heard, touched, felt, or spoken, there is the whole rhythm of the year with its reminder of God's redemptive activity. This is the liturgical calendar which forms the church year. There have been lengthening and shortening of seasons, variety in the observances of times, changes in the celebration of days, but in its present form the Christian year is found helpful by a large segment of Christendom. The Christian year begins on the first Sunday in Advent — the time of the preparation for the coming of the Lord. Advent is a time of solemn expectation. Its hymns include " O Come, O Come, Emmanuel" (twelfth century) and " Come, Thou Long-expected Jesus " (Charles Wesley). Collects and Scripture readings are reminders of John the Baptist's announcing the coming of Christ, and the Bible's witnessing to his coming and to his coming again in judgment and in glory. Each season has a color to fit its mood. For Advent it is violet, symbolic of repentance and preparation for the coming of the Son of God.

Christmas, with its stories of Bethlehem, bursts forth in dazzling, shining white on December 25, and is celebrated until January 6, when Epiphany announces the visit of the Wise Men. The Eastern Church has continued an ancient usage in celebrating Epiphany as the Feast of the Nativity rather than the earlier December 25. Epiphany is the Feast of the Incarnation. The Epiphany season is clothed in green, and its gospel stories revolve around the signs by which God manifested his presence among men in Jesus Christ: the boy Jesus sitting among the teachers in the Temple, Christ proclaiming the gospel, changing water into wine, stilling the storm at sea, healing and forgiving the paralytic.

Lent also is a time of repentance and preparation. Three pre-Lenten Sundays have been added, preceding Ash

Wednesday ("Ashes to ashes" and "Rend your hearts
and not your garments"). We, too, are implicated in the
awful event toward which the days and weeks are moving.
On Passion Sunday, we remember that Jesus set his face
toward Jerusalem; on Palm Sunday the solemnly trium-
phal entrance to Jerusalem is recalled. The four Gospel
accounts of the passion are recited, beginning on Palm
Sunday. Tradition has found many ways to enhance and
deepen the mood of the week. The cross is veiled in violet,
seen only faintly through its translucent covering. There
are no flowers in the sanctuary. The Tenebrae services in
midweek alternate the reading of psalms with the extinguishing of candles, suggesting the flight of the apostles and
the momentary departure of the Light of the World. On
Maundy Thursday the mood changes and the altar is
clothed in white. This rejoicing marks the institution of
the event by which the Lord gave to his people the central
act of their worship. It signifies his living presence, and
his coming again, even as it points to the remembrance of
his passion and death. The feast ends. The Lord of the feast
has gone into the night — to his lonely vigil in the Garden,
to his trial, and to his death. His people wait with him in
sorrow, reliving the event. Varied liturgical services have
grown up through which Christian people express their
devotion during Holy Week. The Good Friday Three
Hours' Service, still popular in many churches, stems from
a medieval practice. The *tre ore* is mainly a listening service. More congregational participation is possible through
a service that uses a dramatic reading of the passion narrative, where readers in the chancel take the roles of Jesus,
Peter, Pilate, and the narrator, while the congregation find
themselves answering in the words of the mob, "Crucify
him." The litany might follow. The Roman Catholic
Church has reestablished the celebration of the Eucharist
at this service, enunciating the significance of the day, however, by omitting the canon of the Mass, since to re-present

the sacrifice on the day when the church is commemorating it would be unseemly and repetitive.

There follows an interval of quiet while the church awaits in solemn expectancy the return of the Lord. The Easter Saturday rites move toward a midnight celebration that ushers in the joyous day. Since Baptism is the rite of resurrection, the water to be used in Baptism is blessed, as well as oil to be used for anointing, symbol of the work of the Holy Spirit. A new fire is kindled from a flint, symbol of the new life. The church which has been dark and silent from the close of Maundy Thursday until this moment begins to come alive. The cross, veiled in black for Good Friday, is made manifest again; the white cloth of Easter is laid on the Table. The candles are lighted with a taper started at the new fire. The tall paschal candle is ceremoniously lighted and affixed to a place next to the baptismal font. The lights in the church blaze forth with the candles; the organ peals out: " Christ the Lord is risen today. Alleluia! " Flowers complete the symbols of the resurrection. Throughout Christendom hymns, flowers, and light shout the glad good news. The Easter season has come. For forty days the church will recall the narratives of the risen Lord: the supper at Emmaus, the empty tomb, the appearance in the upper room, the appearance by the lake, and finally the departure of Jesus from their sight — forty days in which to enjoy the whiteness, to sing the Easter hymns, and to assure one another, " Christ is risen! "

Ascension Day is followed ten days later by the third major feast day of the Christian year — Pentecost — recalling the gift of the Holy Spirit. (The color is red, symbolizing the tongues of flame, the color likewise for saints and martyrs.)

The following Sunday, Trinity, ushers in the long season in which the church is constantly reminded that God is at work in the world through Christians, and the emphasis is on the Christian life. The color is green, said to symbolize creation. The traditional dating of the calendar was to number the Sundays after Pentecost (the Lutherans follow the Western Catholic tradition in this). The Anglican tradition has numbered the Sundays from Trinity Sunday. American denominations, upon adopting the use of the church year, have tended to follow the latter tradition, but seem to be turning to the former and older one. This cycle of remembrance every year makes recurrent the story of God's redeeming action told in the New Testament.

Each Sunday is a little Easter, a remembrance of the resurrection. It is a day of rejoicing, a feast day, even during Lent. This is why the Eucharist has been a strong tradition for Sunday worship, emphasizing as it does the presence of the risen Christ. It should not be confused with the Sabbath of Judaism, which was traditionally a day of rest as well as of worship. The first Jewish Christians observed the Sabbath and held their own times of worship on Sunday. Since the Greco-Roman Christians had to work on Sunday, it was not a day of rest for them. In some periods Protestant Christianity has tried to combine the two and has frequently come out with a solemn day of duty which overcame the earlier weekly celebration of the resurrection. This may be why American Christians today are not really sure how to observe Sunday — what is recreation and what is work, and which (if either or both) belong with the day. The Christian tradition can tell us only that it always has been a day that began with worship. (Education as a Sunday activity is a much later addition, beginning with Robert Raikes in the late eighteenth century.)

Christians are not agreed as to what special days should be celebrated. Early Christian congregations celebrated the birthday into eternal life of their martyrs. As the church became recognized, the days became stablilized and they also multiplied. Each region had its own heroes. The Reformation found the church with a multiplicity of holidays, which was fine for the workers but hard on the work. Luther abolished many, and the liturgical Protestant churches kept those dates which referred to Biblical events (the transfiguration, the annunciation, etc.) and to the apostles. Much of Protestantism dropped all such holy days (the New England Puritans even dropped Christmas). People seem to need holidays if not holy days. The Protestant calendar is filled with special Sundays that attempt to put Christian values into secular events: Mother's Day, Labor Sunday, etc. The older Christian calendar emphasizes God's actions, whereas newer inventions emphasize man's responsibility: Youth Sunday, Race Relations Sunday, Brotherhood Sunday, and the like. These are questionable observances today, for sensitive Christians realize that these concerns should be exercised throughout the year. Holidays are dramatic reminders of religious events, and call the Christian to join with the rest of the community in celebrating what God has done for them.

The vestments worn by those who officiate at a service have their own symbolic value. The Geneva robe has been worn by clergy in the Reformed tradition, emphasizing the scholarly background for the preaching of the Word. The surplice and cassock, as well as the Eucharistic vestments, emphasize the priestly function and the celebration of the Sacrament. The Eucharistic garments echo the colors of the day and season, and suggest the special quality of the event (they, like all vestments, become modified by changing usages in dress). Even the black suit and black tie are a significant form of ministerial dress, suggesting a layman who has a specific function for this occasion (who else wears a black tie with a business suit?). Choir robes usually have conformed to the garments of the clergy: when Geneva gowns are worn, the choir also wear long black robes; where more priestly vestments are worn, the choir wear cassock and cotta (a short surplice).

What will the layman wear, now that the new traditions are giving him responsibility for reading the lessons? Protestant churches have preferred uniformity in the chancel and attired them in black robes. Catholic usage emphasizes the role of the layman by having him come forward from the congregation to read a lesson, returning to the same place when he is finished. Customs arise and change, take on new meanings, or revert to the old. The expression of worship is dynamic.

EDUCATION AND THE SIGNS FOR WORSHIP

Signs have immediate educational value in the service of worship. As works of art and as skilled crafts, they express the gift given to the artisan and are his thanksgiving. They are not directly involved in the worship of the congregation but are aids to worship. They are used for the fulfillment of liturgical actions (bread, wine), and are ways of recalling Biblical and historical events.

Education such as this is useful for all. The young and the noneducated (or the noneducable) can learn through sensory means — through the eye, ear, and sense of touch. The child learns the rhythm of the church year simply by seeing its weekly reenactment and asking questions about what he sees or does not see. " Why is the color red? " " Why is the cross covered? " Thus by an ancient method of learning, the child asks of someone he knows — parent or teacher — and the answer can be given immediately. An association develops between object and event, reinforced year by year. Such learning is not easily forgotten. The educated do not find this naïvely simple, for the change has a function. The culturally-minded find appeal in beautiful appointments, whether simple or elaborate. What the educated in their sophistication find objectionable is not simplicity but oversimplification, not beauty but prettiness, not symbolic action but action in order to create aesthetic effect or to enhance a person. They see through the sentimental image, the too ornate carving, the too pretty robes, the harshly colored glass. The signs of worship largely employ the visual arts. These must be used with all the knowledge that informs the choice of music. Only the best is adequate for the worship of God. A mistaken zeal condemns the beautiful church in the poor village. The church was an act of devotion (although some complained of the cost), and it brings the worshipers the opportunity of pausing amid beauty to renew their strength. Rather condemn the middle-class church that looks for bargains for God, and will settle for innocuous architecture, second-rate materials (sturdy but not luxurious, so that they will wear well), and mass-produced objects. Strange is the faith of those who maintain high cultural standards for their own houses while holding a doctrine of mediocrity for the church building!

Although the meaning of most signs is easily apparent, congregations need to have each pointed out in order that they may see the relationship between the object and the act. By written or spoken words, or a conducted visit (frequently used with children), they can be helped to understand how the size and shape and position of Communion table, pulpit, and baptistry reveal the meaning of the rite for their tradition. Symbols need interpretation, whether they appear in a window or in chancel carvings. A common practice in children's curriculum is to suggest that a class spend a session looking at the visual aspects of the church with someone (preferably the minister) as guide. Similar visits could be arranged occasionally for adults after the church service. The intent of such an occasion would be to explain the theological and liturgical significance of the furnishings rather than to tell interesting stories about the history of the building.

A distinction needs to be made between liturgical art and religious art. As in music, whatever is directly useful for the liturgy is liturgical: the altar and its appointments, the pulpit, the Bible, and the windows (because their subjects were chosen to illumine the meaning of Bible and liturgy). Religious art is a broader category, covering most of the religious paintings and sculptures found in museums. Liturgical art from ancient and medieval ruins finds its way into museum collections. Religious art well might be used in other parts of the church building. Great religious and liturgical art exists only in times when the church is willing to recognize talent, put it to use, and pay for the results.[39] This is the only way to encourage such developments. Today the Christian church is entering a new era of liturgical art because the liturgy is being freshly interpreted in contemporary terms through austerely beautiful buildings and objects. Religious art, too, is beginning to reappear, both in paintings (Chagall, Rouault, Manassier) and in sculpture (Epstein, Moore). Some of the most dramatic expressions of contemporary liturgical Christian art are to be found throughout St. Michael's Cathedral, Coventry, England.[40]

If children are to become adults who appreciate the finest in art as the expression of a gift of God, they must have access to such art from their earliest years, and be helped to find how this can bring them more fully into the worship of God. God has made it possible for people to learn through five senses. To omit the expression of worship through any of these ways is to neglect avenues to fuller knowledge.

CHAPTER 8 | # YOUNG MEMBERS PARTICIPATING IN WORSHIP

COMMON WORSHIP implies participation by all members of the church. If any one age group predominates, if either men or women predominate, the whole people of God are not included. If children are not included, or wish not to be included, the service is constructed for adults. This has happened when the basic orientation has been on intellectual comprehension, stressing a listening to the sermon, or when the appeal has been aesthetic, with elaborate choral music, abstruse symbolism, and unexplained actions. The inclusion of children in congregational worship requires that the service be focused around elements comprehensible to the largest number of people, most of whom are not overly intellectual or aesthetic. This does not imply talking down, oversimplifying, finding a least common denominator, or being mediocre. Simplicity can be awesome in its depth — a baby in a manger, for example.

THE YOUNG AND THE WORSHIPING CONGREGATION

Children can comprehend a service in which the whole congregation participates, for this gives them something to do. They cannot sit still easily for long periods of time. (Adults sit still physically, but their thoughts wander freely, a fact less obvious and therefore less noticeable.) Children can attend to the service when there is action to be seen and heard. Their attention is held when there is movement in the congregation and in the chancel (for moving the eyes is a form of physical motion). A change of pace, a change of voice from speaking to singing — these help to hold their attention and interest.

Even the preschool child finds a place in the service of congregational worship. He likes to be with adults occasionally. This gives him a sense of being a person (children do not always feel that adults consider them so), that he belongs enough to be included. It reinforces his varied family experiences, for here is something that he can do with parents, brothers, and sisters. Moreover, the small child takes his behavioral cues from the adults among whom he worships. He knows how to act appropriately for the occasion by following the actions of those around him. It is important to him (in his own feelings) to be able to do this, for it satisfies his sense of identification with his parents.

Limits are set by his age and corresponding development. He cannot sit still as long as adults can, which is why his outward behavior is better in a service where there are frequent changes of posture. Often he is seated where his feet cannot possibly touch the floor unless there are kneeling cushions or benches to serve as a footstool for him. Sometimes he is placed in the rear or on the side of the church where he cannot really see over the heads of adults to know what is going on in front. Thoughtful adults sit with him close to the front. A child needs proximity in order to become involved in a situation; only adults prefer to sit in the rear of the church. A child's lack of intellectual comprehension is a further limitation on the attention span which he brings to the service. Familiarity will make him feel at home with the rhythm of the service, the changes in mood and pace, but neither hymns, nor Scripture, nor prayers will be within his grasp except at Christmastide.

For these reasons, he will find more joy in the church if he accompanies his family only occasionally, especially at Christmas and Easter, when he can be caught up in the note of joy. Unfortunately for him, this is the time when many adults choose to make their infrequent appearances at worship. No one wishes to offend adults, and it is easier to suggest that children be left at home on such days, " in order that there will be more room for our visitors." If the child is to have participation in worship as an early memory, he should be encouraged to attend during his earliest years. Where the Christmas Eve service has been drawing increasing attendance from older adults, a late afternoon or early evening family service unites all those who for various reasons did not attend at the usual hour. Such services, however, must not be planned *for* children, but must have all the impressive dignity of any other service of the church.

Parents themselves differ as to the age at which they wish to have children accompany them, or how often they think this satisfactory to all. Some children sit quietly on all occasions, simply because to do so is part of their personality structure, while others must thrust out energy in physical forms of twisting, staring, and/or talking. For the sake of surrounding worshipers, the latter had best attend briefly, infrequently, and not be squeezed in too closely to others. Sometimes a child's squirming is infrequent, but arouses apprehension on the part of a parent. If such a parent cannot accept this restlessness, he may need for his own sake to postpone the child's attendance. Some children sit more quietly with other adults than with their parents.

Curricular materials have storybooks that help introduce children to the church and indirectly suggest to parents ways of making this introduction. They picture a situation in which a mother and child stop at the church during the week when they have been out shopping. The child sits in the front of the church, looks around, asks questions of his mother, recalls this as the place where people come on Sunday, and joins with his mother in a simple prayer of thanksgiving. When the child comes on Sunday morning, preparation has already been made. Kindergarten classes frequently visit the church at a time other than the worship service in order to be free to look around and have the furnishings and appointments explained. Lest this tend to make the church seem to be primarily a building, such visits are coupled with story materials to help the child understand that the people with whom he praises God on Sunday are the same ones he meets on various occasions during the week, in school, at stores, or on the neighborhood sidewalks.

When a child enters school at the age of six, he finds himself in a restrained and restraining world. He is in this new environment for five hours each day, five days a week. There are frequent changes of method to hold his attention and give him physical release, but he is definitely in training for a sedentary existence, and one in which mental concentration will be an important factor. To these children the environment of the Sunday morning service is not strange, assuming a high degree of congregational participation. He has more physical coordination and more developed mental habits of attention. Whereas earlier he could listen to stories being read, now he is learning to read. Not only does he read books in which words make sentences and stories, but he also begins to sing, learning words and music of more depth than he understood earlier. The preschool child has begun to cultivate habits of listening. Now he can both listen and respond to questions. These skills stand him in good stead at morning worship. The school-age child is ready for training in worship. That practical phrase, " training in worship," is used deliberately. People need preparation in order to participate in this important activity.

The child needs to practice some of the basic hymns and responses. Newer children's hymnals stress the use of church hymnody. The child needs practice in the responsive nature of parts of the service, such as psalms and versicles. It helps when someone explains to him in a few sentences the gist of the Scripture lessons. He can concentrate more readily if the pastoral prayer is in litany form or composed of brief collects with congregational " Amens." He needs to study with other six-year-olds some meanings for the Lord's Prayer and be given some understanding of the basic threefold structure of the Creed, where that is regularly used. Serious study of such materials will develop later. Second-graders, studying a unit of God's creative work, will catch the meaning of the first article of the Creed, and young children, studying stories of Jesus during Lent will grasp his life events encapsulated in the second section of the Creed. Memorizing comes most easily when it simply happens because one is part of a congregation repeating the same words in a purposeful setting. There is no need deliberately to memorize basic liturgical materials used in unison. When the child can read, he will see these words in print and be able to correct aural misunderstandings.

Sometimes a curriculum is free enough to include such learning within the session plans. When the attendance at the service is assumed, the teaching about the action must come either as preparation before the service or as explication in class after the service. It is also possible to have an extended session if the children leave the service before its end, when, through various methods, they are helped to understand their participation more clearly. Some curricula plan children's church attendance in third or fourth grade, and the corresponding course of study is on worship. At this point participation and explication are brought together. Not all children will be ready or equal to church attendance at this time, although most should be, physically and intellectually. There are children to whom concentration is a problem in any situation. They cannot learn to sit quietly but will unthinkingly disturb other members of the congregation. Someone needs to join them in a classroom activity, not as deprivation or punishment, but simply while awaiting readiness.

Children need special help in understanding the service of worship during the first months that they attend regularly. Whether such attendance should be weekly, biweekly, or monthly is a subject on which there are many opinions. The church school session will be shortened if the service is held at the same time. First-graders are ready to go less frequently than are older children, requiring flexible scheduling in the church school. Seating arrangements in the church become unbalanced when part of the congregation leaves at midpoint. Advocates of family church attendance feel that all members should be present every Sunday, and that with adequate preparation this can be a joyous experience for even the youngest members. Certainly it is important that children sit with their parents or with other adults, for their quiet will be encouraged as they observe the quietness, relaxation, and assurance of the adults about them. When a row of children sit together, the squirming of one child becomes contagious. Ushers sometimes assume that children require less room than adults, with uncomfortable results. The time of the children's departure from the church should not be looked upon as a disturbance. Protestants might well take a cue from the easy informality with which Roman Catholics enter and leave the church, assuming that since others are engaged in worship, their own quiet leaving could hardly be disturbing. The children's leaving can come during a hymn. Some prefer the orderliness of having a children's choir lead a recessional in which children join as they walk up the aisle and out. There is really no necessity for cover-up techniques: when the time comes for this group of worshipers to leave, they simply do so quietly.

Older children (fourth grade and up) should feel quite comfortable in the service of worship. Their musical training enables them to follow in the hymnal with some understanding. They can find meaning in the Scripture lessons. The responses have become familiar. The prayers have meaning. Regular attendance at worship is considered a prerequisite part of the preparation for communicant membership. The question often asked concerning junior high or high school young people is whether they will continue to attend services after they have been confirmed or received as communicants. The answer is not easy. On the one side is a habit that has been building up, supposedly with some meaning. On the other hand, there is the urge to act differently from parents in the quest for personal identity. If "going to church" is regarded as essentially an adult activity, there is an incentive to participate in a fully adult action pattern. Where the relationship to God has been growing in meaning, adolescent devotion can be very strong. In these years, when he begins to know himself as an autonomous person, the adolescent becomes capable of commitment. Belonging to Christ becomes a voluntary act in which love, obedience, and service are intertwined. To such young people, attendance at worship is both a sign and an expression of commitment. The adolescent's faithfulness at common worship reflects how he has understood the meaning of worship. If it has been taught to him as an individual and/or subjective activity, he may prefer to engage in this kind of worship in solitude. If it has been bound up with close associations to others in a common work, he will want to continue the pattern, and may even feel uncomfortable when he is absent. His response may be further bound up with his total sense of what it means to belong and the extent to which morning worship is both a strengthening of him in the hour and a sending of him out into the world. He wants a connection between what happens on Sunday morning and what will happen in high school during the rest of the week.

The adolescent is highly critical of adult ways when these express needs that are foreign to his own life. One cannot imagine the adolescent singing, " Art thou weary, art thou languid? " Some Scripture readings seem overly moralistic. "You listen to this, but you don't really accept it," he would say. Prayers may be introspective, even sentimental. Sermons frequently reflect the needs the pastor has found in older adults. Seldom do illustrations suggest that failure is a problem in high school as well as at work, that inter-personal problems arise between parents and children as well as between husbands and wives, that social problems involve young and old. Adolescents often feel that adults want the church to reinforce in the young the moral codes which the adults are unable to fulfill themselves, whether these be work habits, success goals, or sexual relationships. Such matters should be spoken of to young and old alike in the light of man's sinful nature and God's redemptive love. Young people also believe that while adults expect them to be present at worship, they are excluded from other areas of participation as being too young.

A service will engage the loyal participation of all ages when it is explained and made meaningful. A habit learned young will continue if it has brought satisfying feelings, such as being with parents, being comfortably quiet, seeing color and motion, listening to a familiar voice. This is the point of conditioned learning: that ac-tions which are " rewarded " with pleasurable responses tend to be repeated and reinforced and thus to become in-ternalized. The opposite is also possible. If the memory is one of discomfort — that of feeling Mother rigid or Dad impatient, of slow music and of incomprehensible words, of the ache from a head bowed too long — these responses also become reinforced until the day when the unpleasant activity can be avoided. Joy is the keynote on which a deep and meaningful participation in the life of the worshiping community will grow.

CHURCH SCHOOL WORSHIP

The church school grew up in the United States as a parallel activity to the regular work of the church, with separate personnel, budget, and materials. While people might attend both Sunday morning worship and church school (traditionally called Sunday school), there was not until relatively recent years any thought of correlation. In such a system, church school worship could easily be assumed alongside the worship of the church. In the distant past, this took the form of opening exercises, presided over by a general superintendent in the presence of everyone from the youngest child (the Beginners Department started with the four-year-olds) to the oldest member of the adult class. The mainstay of these exercises was congregational singing, often chosen on the spot ("What would you like to sing today? ") or in a brief consultation with the pianist just before the opening ("What hymns do you know? "). There would be a reading of Scripture and usually a talk by the superintendent. The minister would offer the morning prayer. Then the collection would be taken.

The rise of religious education as a discipline related to general education aroused a concern that this opening should be meaningful to each participant, and that it should become a worship service. If the former was to happen, there would have to be a breakdown of the all-inclusive assembly. The preschoolers were the first to be granted their own separate assembly, followed by the primaries. This happened when teachers, newly informed through emerging teacher training conferences, found various means to persuade the superintendent to give up part of his congregation. The development of graded curriculum materials helped the cause, for these began to include departmental worship materials. Further encouragement came from the interdenominational agency, the International Council of Religious Education, through its monthly magazine, the *International Journal of Religious Education*, which contained a section of worship materials for each age group. Soon juniors, intermediates, and seniors were each having separate services. The graded worship service was an accomplished fact in all but the smallest rural church schools.

One criterion was now accomplished: the groups were sufficiently limited age-wise that the material could be geared to the understanding of all. The second criterion was that this should become a service of worship, so that each child and young person could participate meaningfully in the basic service of worship of the church. The first concern was for form: it should follow the pattern used at morning worship — call to worship, hymn, Scripture, prayers, offering, and a story talk as equivalent to the sermon. Such a service might be as brief as ten minutes for the kindergarten and as long as half an hour for juniors and young people. There was a concern for the quality of the hymnody, leading to a drastic change in the quality of children's hymnals as more church hymns were introduced. Words of hymns followed the prevailing trends in the adult hymnals, whether didactic, social-action, or theological.

Next the setting became important. Sometimes this resulted in the building of children's chapels, some scaled to three-year-olds. These seemed charming to adults, but were too formal for little children. The general chapel was more functional, being regularly used for weddings, funerals, evening services, and Communion services. This became a real place of worship and not a setting contrived for a weekly ten-minute children's service. To such a chapel groups could go for the departmental worship service. The grades included in a single service were usually determined by the seating capacity of the chapel and the departmental organization of the church school. The department superintendent, who understood the children involved, became the responsible leader, assisted by teachers and sometimes by selected children. Where no such chapel was available, "worship centers" appeared in classrooms. Church schools have been known to have such worship centers securely fastened to the wall of each room, complete with cross and candles, flowers and Bible. The purpose was to provide an orderly setting for worship similar to that which the children would find in the church.

Church and church school still did not work congruently. Churches with central pulpits were setting up worship tables in classrooms; churches celebrating the Lord's Supper weekly had imitation altars in classrooms which never saw a Communion service. The intention was good; the results were something less than perfect. The setting became an imitation of the church, the service a substitute for morning worship; the children were effectively cut off from the congregation at worship. The attempted plan had merit, given the background of early twentieth-century Protestant worship nearing the end of the great era of prima donna preachers who focused worship on the sermon. This had little to say to children, although in small churches the sense of belonging and family attendance had its own value despite some lack of intelligibility.

Currently, the formal departmental worship service is less emphasized. The setting becomes informal. The worship center is simpler, choosing among the variety of possible accouterments. A children's congregation that meets together for worship is not in any sense competitive to or in imitation of the morning service, which alone is the climax of the Sunday celebration. Hymns, prayers, Scripture, and offering are included, but the stress is on mutual sharing in praise and thanksgiving to God. The time is shortened. The purpose of the brief church school hour is primarily for study, and teachers already are trying frantically to adapt a full curriculum to the allotted time. Preschool classes put the emphasis on informality, using simple songs with words of joyous thanksgiving, a few Biblical verses, brief prayer. This comes when play activities are ended and the group gathers for the quieter activities of song and story. There should be no feeling of compulsion to have this time of worship every week. There will be days when the children are either overactive or overtired, conditions scarcely conducive to worship. Some children's leaders insist that the service for preschool children, although brief, should be held in an especially planned setting. They point out that children enjoy ceremony, find order satisfying, and need assurance of participation in an adult type of activity preparatory to joining their parents in the "big church." For such an order, something like the following can be used:

Quiet music
Call to worship (a Biblical verse of praise)
Hymn of praise
Scripture verses
Prayer
Offering
Hymn
Blessing

Some teachers want to use more of the surroundings of the formal service. They say, "Children enjoy the glow of candles, attention is focused, and they need this way of serving." So they put a big hand over the child's little one, guiding him through the intricacies of putting taper to candle. Then at the end they give similar help to the child who wields the candle snuffer. Actually, children do not appreciate that kind of adult assistance, nor are they under any illusion that they are really lighting the candles. (Try to dress a three-year-old who is determined to do it himself!)

It is safe to say, however, that a child is not ready to perform such an action until he can do it unaided. This holds true when primary-age children are asked to take leadership roles in the service. Such a service is usually a source of disquietude among the teachers, and of meaninglessness to the children, when a child leader falters through a reading he does not understand or a prayer he has not read previously. Leading others in worship is a serious responsibility and should be entered into seriously. Doubtless some children are capable of leading, but even they should be entrusted with the task only after careful preparation. A teacher will want to help them study the meaning and practice the words until parts of the service can be read or recited fluently and with comprehension. If this kind of rehearsal suggests a performance rather than a service, it would be well to reflect on the fact that ministers do this mentally as part of their preparation, and that only the week-by-week reenactment across months and years makes it possible for them to lead with such ease that they and their people worship together. An untrained person, child or adult, cannot act with less preparation. When a service is a dialogue between leader and congregation, with unison hymns, prayers, and responses, the people are participating as fully (literally, in terms of speech and action) as is the leader. Children do not have to be leaders, i.e., initiators, in the service in order to be participants.

The trend toward including children and young people fully and frequently in the basic congregational service of worship has caused questions to be raised with regard to the purpose and place of the departmental worship service. Habit-bound superintendents have been known to hold a departmental service for primary children who come directly from the church service. For what reason? No one sends the adults to an afterchurch service. Nor can one give adequate rationale for a departmental worship service with juniors, junior highs, and senior highs, who are able to understand the full service of morning worship. Their time is more needed for classroom study. Sometimes the departmental service is a substitute for attendance at morning worship. It may be a matter of scheduling: they cannot attend morning worship because there are no plans for teaching after they leave the service. Their parents bring them for one hour and are unwilling to leave them for a second hour. Their attention span is limited to one hour. The first two objections are valid in some situations. The attention span, as schoolteachers know, varies with the degree of involvement of the child in an absorbing or tedious situation.

There may be real reason for a simple preschool service, and even for a primary service on days when that group does not attend morning worship, but a junior department service is more open to question. At this age the first rebellion against church school attendance frequently discloses that the girls are more decorous in their behavior than are the boys. Teachers frequently aim the service at the younger children, with the result that hymns and prayers may seem " childish " to older boys and girls, and a story aimed at one segment hits none. A class worship committee will not necessarily improve the situation. They know the kind of services teachers expect them to plan. Junior boys and girls are ready for serious study of the elements of congregational worship. They need neither substitutes nor imitations. A simple act of worship at the beginning and/or the end of the session is sufficient. This could be a prayer said either in unison, by a member of the group, or by a teacher, praising God for his presence and praying for the guidance of his Spirit in their work.

Classes made up of children from a singing tradition in school or community (or where members belong to a children's choir) might use one stanza of a hymn, learning one for each season — Advent, Christmas, Epiphany, Lent, Passiontide, Easter, and Pentecost. At the close of the session a blessing may be spoken by all in unison or by one in behalf of all. Where a particular course of study is based on specific Biblical material, the section to be used that day might be read devotionally at the opening of the session. Thus it would be heard first within the framework of worship, and later commented upon in terms of its distinctive setting and meaning.

What is said here concerning young people applies equally well to adult groups. There is no reason to open a church school session with a full-blown worship service unless the members considered this to be their church service and did not join the rest of the community for worship. Such a group would definitely have cut themselves off from the main worshiping body for reasons of their own!

The same criteria apply to evening and weekday groups: men's club, women's society, mothers' club, etc. These are groups meeting variously for fellowship, work, and/or study. It may be assumed that the worship service has become a mere formality if people start coming late to the meeting (in order to miss it?). An opening act of worship needs simply to be a prayer by which the group remembers before God that they are a fellowship within the whole people of God gathered for mutual strengthening and witness. When an evening service is regularly held on Sunday, scheduled groups might well begin or conclude their meetings by participating in it. Similarly, a weekday group that meets close to the time of a regular weekday service might well share in it. Groups that begin with supper might attend a five-thirty vesper service or end with the midweek service. Such a range of services is found normally only in larger churches or in city settings, but the possibilities even elsewhere are considerable. Clergymen are usually eager to cooperate in the arranging of corporate services of worship, especially when a certain group will be known to provide a core attendance.

This is contrary, of course, to a point of view that looks upon the worship service as an aid to the consolidation of the group. Mutual worship can indeed help knit the bonds that bind people in loving concern. But it does not necessarily perform this function. The Sunday evening high school group, for example, is volatile. No one, neither they nor their leaders, really knows how they will "feel" on a particular evening. Their discussion might lead them into prayer. Then again, worship of any kind might be an imposition involving them only in irreverent behavior that will discomfit them upon later recollection. This is why leaders of youth usually prefer to keep the plans flexible. When some of the young people themselves ask for a regularly scheduled worship service, why do they do so? Do they think that this gives them an "in" with the establishment? Or, more kindly, does this reinforce identifications with the adult leaders? Do they find comfort in the form where they would feel threatened to discuss the reality? (" Who is God? " " How are we related to him? " "What is commitment? ") A formal service with the young people's group, furthermore, could be a substitute for morning worship. (" The young people are up late Saturday night and they don't get up Sunday mornings! " " If we didn't have a carefully planned service at the young people's group, they wouldn't often see a service of worship! ") Perhaps the answer lies in providing a late afternoon or early evening service for all Sunday sleepers!

One adult group takes the study and practice of prayer as its primary function. This group does not need a formally constructed service of worship, although they might open or close with a devotional hymn. Prayer for them is more spontaneous and less directed than in most groups. These persons regard their service as intercession, and through such they are a leaven and a strength to the whole worshiping community. They are less concerned about studying the elements in the liturgy because worship informs all their work.

God is present among his people in all their activities. He is with the kindergarten children at play, with the primary children illustrating a story, with the juniors asking and answering questions, with the high school students in their concerned discussion, with the adults in their varied tasks. The purpose of study for the life of the church is to deepen understanding of God's self-disclosure so that the learner may be strengthened in commitment and be fortified for his life of daily service. Such understanding, arrived at through common study, is conveyed into the worship of the congregation. The learning and responding find place in a different setting, with a different purpose: that God may be glorified among his people. Let nothing that the smaller groups do detract from the common work of each single congregation, which is linked with others throughout the world, with those in the past, and with the whole company of heaven to praise and magnify God's glorious name.

CHAPTER 9 | # WORSHIP AND WITNESS

S INCE WORSHIP IS THE CENTER for the life of the Christian community, the questions that arise from people are best seen in this light and with this background. How can one speak about God except as he is known through the experience of the congregation?

THE QUESTIONS ASKED

A child learns about God from many sources. A radio program later transcribed in a record indicates this.[41] " Where did you first hear about God? " the children are asked. They answer: " From my mother "; " My grandmother told me "; " One day in the park the children were talking about God." The early understanding of God is derived from what parents say and from what they do. They may teach a child to pray before they explain why or to whom prayer is addressed. The child may participate in some form of family worship — at meals, in the evening, or on special occasions. A parent may refer to God in order to reinforce orders: " God does not want you to do this." The child's understanding reflects the content and occasions for prayer and the reinforcement of conduct. These come in for reflection and correction when the child participates in the service of worship.

Whether this is a service for preschool children or the morning worship of the whole congregation, the child is confronted with certain assumptions expressed in hymns, Scripture readings, prayer, and the mood of the service. If this service is the fullest way in which the church knows how to express its understanding of and relationship to God, then it becomes the norm and point of reference by which religious questions can be answered.

The church at worship is a people who believe in God and assume that he is present in their midst. This assurance is carried to the child, who responds to what he senses in the adults. It needs no verbal explanation. The nature of the understanding of God is made clear when joy, praise, and thanksgiving predominate. The affirmation of the providential love of God is brought out through participation in intercessory prayer. The fellowship with the present Lord is made known in the Supper. When the child asks, " Who made God? " he is answered, " We know nothing before God; we gather in his presence and see how his love is made known, and we are assured that he is real " (for the child is asking about reality). When the older child says, " Do you believe all these stories in the Bible? " he is answered that the Bible tells the story of God's action through many literary forms — hymns, stories and teaching, letters, historical chronicles — all of which are used in the service (the child is inquiring about the relation of truth to fact). Fullness of understanding is many-sided. One becomes aware of how the Biblical material is used in the service: the choice of readings, the preaching, selections from the psalms. The answer to the child is illumined by pointing to such factors. Some parts of the Bible have more value for the community, as is evidenced in the choice of passages read and explained at the gathering for worship. Other portions are used in study or used illustratively, and some are omitted. The older child learns the criteria for selectivity.

The service evokes questions before answering them. It is not philosophical, nor does it theorize. It is action. The purpose is not to answer questions but to affirm and act upon understood convictions about the relationship between God and his people. The service asks the participant to look at the meaning of prayer by praying, and so to become aware of the kind of relationships presupposed and expressed. The language used, the forms employed, the emphases of thanksgiving and of petition developed, suggest their own answers. The child, the questioning young person, and the questing adult sense the affirmations being made through such action, and find themselves asking questions about God, who is addressed. Why do we assume that God hears? What is the nature of a God who hears and responds? What do we feel we may ask or not ask? What are the limits of God's responsibility and those of the worshiper? How do we respond in the face of unanswered prayer? How can we praise in times of distress? Note that the questions raised are response to and reflection of what the words and actions have said implicitly, rather than what has been spoken explicitly.

The service suggests questions concerning the understanding of Jesus Christ and his place within worship, for it is he who makes Christian worship distinctive from that of the other two monotheistic faiths. Some services do not meet this test. They express a " Jesus religion," or they suggest the possibility of two Gods and a Holy Spirit which is an " it." The service of worship should clearly make known the Christian understanding of God revealed in Christ, present and acting as Holy Spirit. Christian worship expresses this unique understanding of God. Attempts to define God as Trinity in intellectual terms lead only to abstruseness, conflicts, and counterclaims, beginning with the long-fought-over Creed of Nicaea and brought sharply into focus in the theology of the moment. Attempts to explain God in such theoretical terms to young people or adults is unsatisfactory. Some apprehension of the fullness of God can be felt and expressed through the liturgy, which praises God by name, affirms his coming in Jesus Christ through the words of the Creed and the ending to its prayers, assumes his presence in the Eucharist, and sends the people forth with the promise of his Spirit. The deepest understandings of life are never fully explainable. If God could be explained, defined, and thereby limited, he would become subject to human power, and this would not be God. Obviously, such is impossible. The service suggests the question, Who is the God here addressed and celebrated? and answers through the words of hymn, prayer, Scripture, and the canon of the Sacrament.

The service also asks and answers questions about the nature of the church. These people gathered together in the presence of God call themselves the church. The nature of the church is being demonstrated (not defined) in dimensions that are human as well as divine. One is aware of relationships among the people and of the assembly's sense of relationship to God. The nature of the church is expressed in the way the people assemble and in how they leave; in their manner of participation and in the variety of persons present. Such demonstration raises questions, best answered with reference to this primary function of the church.

Some people do not attend church, or they attend in accordance with personal inclination. Is the church then basically an organization? Is it an accumulation of groups? Is it an agency for giving comfort and/or other forms of aid? These questions may be answered partly by reference to how such functions grow out of and are expressive of the function of worship. Many New Testament images of the church can be explained through worship: the *ekklēsia,* the body of Christ, the covenant community, the branches of which Christ is the vine. These terms describe individuals acting in unison of purpose, word, and action. When the worshiping congregation fails to represent these images, negative questions are raised, questions which should be an embarrassment to the church. Why are there so few people present if this gathering is important? Why are all the people similar in age, social class, or color? Why does the service seem self-centered, emphasizing personal salvation? Why is it sadly a memorial rather than joyfully a celebration? The complexion of the service of worship raises questions in the mind of the inquirer, the newcomer, and the doubter. They say, " This is what we see, but we hear you explain yourself differently." The questions can be more satisfactorily met when there is some attempt at correspondence between the congregation's expressed image of the church in words and its acted-out image both in the service and in other areas of its life.

Questions are raised about the highly symbolic nature of worship. Hymns contain figures of speech, Biblical passages are obscure, prayers — even when informal or spontaneous — include specifically religious phraseology, the offertory is announced in evasive terms, the service moves with an inner but unexplained rhythm. Objects are not simply what they appear to be but have enhanced meanings: The Bible is not just another book; the font is for a special rite seen nowhere else; the table is not a dining room table, although it is used for a " supper "; the cross, which could have many uses as a form composed of two bars at right angles, here takes on endless meanings. Such questions are to be found even in the minds of worshipers. In a culture so imbued with the belief that all problems will find concrete solutions, objects as " odd " and rites as strange as these will surely evoke response. Symbols express reality, but not in a matter-of-fact way. Why is the Bible a big book, expensively bound, set on a special stand, read in a particular tone of voice, translated into rhythmic phrases, and sometimes even carried to its place in procession, preceded by candles? Such questions lead into Biblical study concerning the purpose of the Bible, its message, and how this Word is different from the word in other books.

Is Baptism the thanksgiving of parents, the dedication of a child, the forgiveness of sins, the renewal of life, or reception into the Christian community? The person so constituted that he must have one single, final, unchanging answer will be disappointed. He may choose one of these and cling to it, but it can never be the full answer, for all these meanings are involved in the rite of Baptism: thanksgiving, forgiveness, renewal, reception, and dedication.

The most bewildering questions surround the Lord's Supper. Even those who see the idea of a " memorial " as a simple explanation with New Testament sanction from the Synoptic Gospels have to wrestle with the fact that the New Testament word *anamnēsis* does not mean " memorial " as contemporary American language seems to understand it, but is a bringing of past memory into the living present. When this New Testament idea of " memorial " is invested with mournful solemnity, the whole triumph of Easter is being ignored. Questions reach depth and perplexity when the structure of the service assumes the meeting of the Lord with his people and the question is asked, " In what way is he present? " There is a growing consensus that however useful Platonic or Aristotelian categories may have been for the Renaissance period, they have been decreasingly helpful since the eighteenth century. Nobody today defines matter in terms of substances and accidents. It may be necessary to revert to earlier practice when a common explanation was assumed but no definition made mandatory. Theological method today is descriptive rather than definitive, and attempts at specific definition bring more heat than light. In this as in other areas of the service (the reading of the Scriptures, for example) the affirmation is made that what happens does so objectively and not subjectively. God speaks through the Scriptures whether the worshiper hears him or not; he is present in the Eucharist whether the worshipers "feel" him or not. God's presence is not dependent upon man's response.

The inclusion of so much that is symbolic in the service raises questions about its reality. If one always has to be translating, how has he time to assimilate meaning? The answer may be that symbols are not so much translated as they are apprehended (this is true in the use of a second language: an object simply has two names). The value of the symbol is that meaning can increase — be enhanced and deepened. There is no final or complete response. One says to the child: " In the Lord's Supper we rejoice because Christ is with us, just as we are happy at a family meal at home." Later he will learn about the combinations of sorrow and joy, of death and resurrection, of sin and redemption. The answers to religious questions are not simple, nor are the answers to any of life's deeper questions.

Participation in the worship of the church gives an environment from which to answer questions in a way they cannot be answered for the nonchurch child. Answers given him by parents or teachers regarding the nature of God, the meaning of death, and the reality of evil come from observed human responses in everyday relationships, from history, and from literature. This is good. Worship adds another dimension.

People through religious questions are asking that the service of worship be invested with meaning, or that it come to have meaning for them. They do not accept naïve answers. Unquestioning belief is an exception today where general education has become widespread. Questions may not be voiced, but the reservations can still be present. On the other hand, people do not reason abstrusely: they leave that for the experts. Explanations must be clear and uncluttered, in popular terms. Neither of the two classic Roman Catholic explanations of the real presence is useful: few people are simple enough to be satisfied by " It looks like bread, it tastes like bread, but it is not bread," nor does anyone feel enlightened by the definition that the sub-stance of Christ is contained within the accidents of bread. Protestants have their own equivalents, especially, in the area of theories of the atonement.

A congregation that understands with heart and head can make a deep response in worship, ministering to one another in their praise to God. The questions raised by this participation are important, and the gradual unfolding of answers through word and experience is assuring if not final.

WORSHIP AND SERVICE

There is a saying in some churches: " Enter to worship; depart to serve." The action begun in the gathering together is continued as the members go their separate ways to family, school, and work. When Jesus sent out the Twelve on their mission, it is written that he said, " Behold, I send you out as sheep in the midst of wolves " (Matt. 10:16) . When the risen Lord was about to leave his disciples, he said, " Go therefore and make disciples of all nations " (Matt. 28:19) .

God's gift is his presence in worship and in work. The human response is service for him, a response inseparable from what God does, for the work can only be accomplished through the power of his Holy Spirit. The Christian goes forth with Christ into the world, always endeavoring to find appropriate forms. Wilhelm Hahn has summed this up by saying:

> Therefore both Worship and Sacrifice are at one and the same time God's service to us and our human service to Him. God's service to us and our service to Him permeate one another, and what God does for us he does only in, with, and under our service.[42]

The Christian's service begins with his service within the congregation: as deacon, elder, choir member, church school teacher, committee member, group officer, or fulfilling some work among the many activities of an organization. More important (for the church can exist without organizations) are the forms of mutual help: visiting the sick and the shut-ins, comforting families to which death has come, helping people in times of crisis, giving food, clothing, money, and work as necessary. The Christian congregation should be a large family practicing mutual support and helpfulness. When this is neglected, the vitality of the church is endangered. Some people feel that they should be ashamed of their need, or that they should be able to solve problems unaided. The congregation may be blind toward this necessary service. Members fail to cultivate a mutual openness to give and to receive. The signs of Christ's coming as reported to the disciples of John the Baptist were that " the blind receive their sight and the lame walk, lepers are cleansed and the deaf hear, the dead are raised up, and the poor have good news preached to them " (Matt. 11:5). This work begins with a congregation where Christ is present. Practice enables his people to carry these signs into the world with greater assurance.

Worship can be a comfort to people in distress, can give strength to the weak and courage to the faltering. But true worship does not keep people dependent children, always returning to be fed but never having enough strength to help others. The church dare not be a refuge in the way some mothers' arms are a shield from the world. The refuge is a respite for the recovery of strength. A retreat — whether religious or in battle — is for the purpose of recovery in order to go back to the war. On Sunday morning, people who share conviction and devotion find security in meeting together. What kind of security are they sharing? The church is not meant to be a place to which one runs in the face of threat from an unfriendly world. This can happen to those who hold an unworldly or otherworldly view of Christianity derived from a particular in-

terpretation of " in the world but not of the world." Nor
is it an escape from change. Change is at the very heart of
life itself; anyone tempted to doubt this should look at one
of his own baby pictures. There will be changes in the
physical environment, in society, and in economic life. The
New Testament closes with a great apocalyptic vision of
God's new creation. To expect the church to shield one
from change is to assume that some power other than God
rules the world. The frequency of nostalgic hymns, sermons, and prayers suggests that some Christians believe
this. Whatever else participation in Christian worship does,
it must equip Christians to witness to their faith by their
everyday lives.

This need not be so obvious as explaining to school
friends or business associates what it means to be a Christian, although it could mean that. There are times for revealing the source of one's strength and times for showing
it wordlessly.

Nor does witness carry any suggestion of moralism. It
does not give a mandate to say by word, act, or attitude
that the Christian is the " good " person because he acts
after a certain pattern which other people ought to follow.
People are quick to sense when they are being judged. The
business world is filled with this — the constant weighing
and deciding as to who moves up or down the ladder, to
the branch office or the main office. In such a setting, the
presence of a person who is constantly trying to remake
others under the guise of Christian concern would be un-
bearable. Those who do wrong are sometimes caught in
almost unsolvable dilemmas between a moral equivoca-
tion, which preserves the job to support the family, and a
clear-cut refusal, which can undermine a whole career.
The Christian faith affirms the full humanity of man — in
Augustine's phrase, " at the same time sinners and made
just." Being sinful is part of being human; being made
just is a work that only God can perform. The preacher

who thinks he strengthens his people by telling them that God loves them *in spite of* their wrongdoing, and encourages them to keep raising the standard, misses the whole point of the Biblical understanding of man. God could not love any other kind of man because this is the only kind of human being in existence. Raising the standard leads to hypocrisy as a person subconsciously realizes that the gap between the real and the ideal is daily widening. People find it necessary either to whitewash themselves or to condemn others. Those who rejoice each Sunday in the resurrection life do not need this kind of moralism as a basis for witness. The good news of forgiveness to the repentant needs to be spoken where life is so manifestly imperfect: the place of everyday work. When Jesus prayed for his disciples, " I do not pray that thou shouldst take them out of the world, but that thou shouldst keep them from the evil one " (John 17:15), he did not mean that they should gather into closed groups of purity. They were sent out enabled to maintain love, goodness, and righteousness in the midst of all the evil infiltrating human society. This is an important form of witness.

Christians know that God who broke bread with his people at the joyous feast accompanies them in this less joyful place. The Gospel records tell how Jesus in his earthly life was to be found among the poor, the needy, the sick, and the sinful, as well as among the rich, the religious, and the successful. Christ present through his witnesses confronts this world, offering wholeness and sometimes receiving in response only anger and rejection. Occasionally his word is heard, takes root, and the Christian is enabled to help and to heal. On such occasions he feels blessed, yet he has been equally faithful and equally representative when rejected. There is more difficulty in knowing when rejection results from the attempt at reconciliation, or when personal factors have contributed to this response. One never really knows; the Christian can only offer his life, and rejoice when he is able to be acceptable.

If Christian witness is to be this kind of difficult yet rewarding challenge, worship cannot be simply an inspiration that leaves one with a warm glow. Such feelings are shallow and wear off by Monday morning, or Tuesday at the latest. A form of worship that is common work (*leitourgia*) prepares the worshiper for the uncommon work of the weekday. He may have found the Scripture reading obscure, the prayers may have made him uncomfortable, his mood may have made it difficult fully to participate, but he attended because this witness in the community is the best possible preparation for witness outside the community. When worship itself is work, it imparts strength and courage. Life is affirmed in its fullness: darkness and light, evil and good, hate and love, cowardice and courage. There is always the remembrance of Jacob's wrestling with the angel until he received a blessing and the new name, Israel. He was lamed by the encounter, yet strengthened and made a new man. To worship in the Christian congregation is to believe the words spoken: " Go forth in peace: the blessing of God . . . be with you all." Christ is not localized on any altar. The Holy Spirit dwells in the sanctuary, but also goes forth into every home, every school, and every place of daily work.

Worship that leads to witness gives a sense of solidarity. We are not alone. This contributes to the intense devotion to be found in the worship of a persecuted church. The gathering together cannot be taken for granted. Any day it might be forbidden, the group broken up, members arrested. The solidarity and strength to be garnered from being together is infinitely precious because so insecure, so unpredictable. When the day comes that they are forcibly scattered, there will be the remembrance, the anamnesis, the representation of that common worship. Although in separate imprisonments, they will be gathered together on the Lord's Day, much as John in solitary confinement on the Isle of Patmos felt himself in the Spirit with the seven churches of Asia, surrounded by angels and archangels and all the company of heaven. This realization is lost when Sunday observance and the neighborhood church can be taken for granted. " Shall we go or not go? " is a dilettante question, indifferently made and answered for superficial reasons. A person is rarely so busy, so sleepy, or so sick that he cannot really attend worship; nor is the weather so bad, the distance so far, the transportation so poor that he might not arrive. When being a Christian in daily life is serious business wherein one feels responsible to God, being present in the company at worship is an equally serious necessity.

Worship grants the person a pause: for reflection on what God has done for his people across the generations as well as what he has done and is doing for this one person, and for the response of yielding love in adoration and thanksgiving. Such a reflection provides strength and courage to look forward toward the difficult work of the week, the problematical decisions, and the uncertain situations. Worship gives constant renewal. This is why worship is the basis for witness and why Christian living cannot really take place without it. The solitary Christian does not exist, and there is indeed no salvation outside the church, for within the solidarity of the worshiping congregation bound by the strength of the Holy Spirit salvation is realized. The Christian is not alone even when he exists in a situation of moral or physical solitude.

The congregation in faith and courage dares complete its Eucharistic worship with the prayer that we may " do all such good works as thou has prepared for us to walk in." That which God has prepared, he will fulfill.

◈ ◈ ◈ | NOTES

1. Gerhard Delling notes in *Worship in the New Testament* (Ch. IV) that the form of the letter suggests a possible structure for worship. Helpful material in this area is also developed by C. F. D. Moule, *Worship in the New Testament.*

2. Delling, *op. cit.*, pp. 119 f.

3. This action is frequently called the " shape " of the liturgy, a reference to the use of this fourfold outline by Dom Gregory Dix in *The Shape of the Liturgy.*

4. Bard Thompson, ed., *Liturgies of the Western Church,* p. 9. With its introductions and full translations of the extant Western liturgies, this is a useful book for study.

5. Cf. *The Lord's Day Service* (United Church of Christ, 1964); *Service Book and Hymnal of the Lutheran Church in America* (Augsburg Publishing House, 1958); *The Book of Worship for Church and Home* (Methodist Publishing House, 1965); *The Book of Common Worship: Provisional Services and Lectionary for the Christian Year* (The Westminster Press, 1966); *The Liturgy of the Lord's Supper* (Protestant Episcopal Church, 1966).

6. Paul S. Minear, ed., *Faith and Order Findings* (The Final Report of the Theological Commissions to the Fourth World Conference on Faith and Order, Montreal, 1963); also, Massey H. Shepherd, Jr., ed., *Worship in Scripture and Tradition* (Essays by Members of the Theological Commission on Worship, North American Section, of the Commission on

Faith and Order of the World Council of Churches).

7. See Bibliography, Sec. IV, " Liturgy in Denominational Traditions."

8. Jean-Jacques von Allmen, *Worship: Its Theology and Practice*, p. 54.

9. Cf. H. A. Williams, " Psychological Objections " in *Objections to Christian Belief* (J. B. Lippincott, 1964).

10. J. G. Davies, G. F. Cope, and D. A. Tytler, *An Experimental Liturgy.*

11. From the Roman Mass and the Lutheran liturgy.

12. Roy S. Lee, *Psychology and Worship*, p. 18.

13. This is more fully developed in two books written for parents and teachers on religious development: Roy S. Lee, *Your Growing Child and Religion: A Psychological Account* (The Macmillan Company, 1963), Chs. 5 to 7; and Marc Oraison, *Love or Constraint?: Some Psychological Aspects of Religious Education,* tr. by Una Morrissy (The Paulist Press, 1961), Ch. 4. Basic categories used are those explored by Erik H. Erikson in several of his writings.

14. Lee, *Psychology and Worship*, p. 54.

15. Hervé Carrier, *The Sociology of Religious Belonging*, pp. 54 f.

16. *Ibid.*, p. 58.

17. The role of the religious leader of a local group is in itself a subject for study. He may be trained (according to varied understandings of the term) or untrained, paid or unpaid, full time or part time, ordained or unordained. His status derives from society as well as from the particular group he serves. His authority varies according to the beliefs of the group. Both the kind and degree of authority have psychosociological as well as religious roots.

18. Cf. the writings of Marshall McLuhan in the field of communications, such as *The Gutenberg Galaxy: The Making of Typographic Man* (University of Toronto Press, 1962) and *Understanding Media: The Extensions of Man* (McGraw-Hill Book Company, Inc., 1964).

19. Cf. the catalogue of the American Bible Society (1865 Broadway, New York, N.Y. 10023), for helpful materials. Individual books from the Bible may be had in paperback at minimal cost. The New Testament is available inexpensively

in attractive paperback formats, in the Revised Standard Version and also in a simplified translation.

20. " The free spontaneous petitionary prayer of the natural man exhibits the prototype of all prayer " (Friedrich Heiler, *Prayer; A Study in the History and Psychology of Religion* [Oxford University Press, 1932], p. 1).

21. *The Book of Common Prayer,* p. 595.

22. A litany of thanksgiving will be found useful in some forms of service, particularly one planned for the purpose of giving thanks at a commemorative event, or during a time for thanksgiving in a prayer service, or by a prayer group. In the usual Sunday worship, however, thanksgiving is expressed in other forms; hence, the litany belongs more appropriately at the point of intercessory or petitionary prayer.

23. John A. T. Robinson, *Honest to God* (The Westminster Press, 1963), pp. 91–97.

24. Helpful prayers in this vein may be found in books such as *Prayers,* by Michel Quoist, tr. by A. M. Forsyth and A. M. de Commaille (Sheed & Ward, Inc., 1963); *Are You Running with Me, Jesus?* by Malcolm Boyd (Holt, Rinehart and Winston, Inc., 1965); and *The Prayer of All Things,* by Pierre Charles, tr. by James Langdale (Herder & Herder, Inc., 1964).

25. John B. Coburn, " A Contemporary Mood: Some Issues and Questions About Prayer," in *Theological Education,* Summer, 1966. The contents of this issue are also found in book form under the title *Horizons of Theological Education: Essays in Honor of Charles L. Taylor,* ed. by John B. Coburn, Walter D. Wagoner, and Jesse H. Ziegler (American Association of Theological Schools, 1966). The book by Dr. Coburn referred to is *Prayer and Personal Religion* (Layman's Theological Library, The Westminster Press, 1957).

26. Hans Urs von Balthasar, *Prayer,* p. 12.

27. *Sing for Joy,* ed. by Norman and Margaret Mealy (The Seabury Press, Inc., 1961), has a section listing hymns or parts of hymns and the age for which they might be usable. References are to *The Hymnal* (1940) of the Protestant Episcopal Church. *Songs and Hymns for Primary Children* (The Westminster Press, 1963) uses many church hymn tunes. *Sing Unto the Lord, Ye Children,* by William Grime (Carl Fischer, Inc., 1965), is a noteworthy collection of original songs.

28. The Lutheran Church in America has provided such a children's edition. There is also a leader's edition that prints the children's page (single clef) on the left side and the full accompaniment (plus background and musical helps) on the facing page.

29. Two such settings are *Rejoice,* made by students of The General Theological Seminary (Episcopal) in New York, and the *Twentieth Century Folk Mass,* by Geoffrey Beaumont.

30. Much of the work in this area has been done in the research and writing of Erik Routley (see the Bibliography).

31. There are also chronological indexes and general background articles on hymnody and congregational singing.

32. Cf. Dix, *op. cit.,* mentioned also in Chapter I.

33. H. G. Hardin, J. D. Quillian, Jr., and J. F. White, *The Celebration of the Gospel: A Study in Christian Worship.*

34. *The Book of Common Prayer,* p. 83.

35. The Lutheran Church in America and the Episcopal curricula have such books. Covenant Life Curriculum (Presbyterian Church in the U.S., and several other denominations) has a reading book to explain the morning service.

36. Published by John Knox Press. Publication began in 1958, and fourteen volumes were in print in 1966. See also, *Studies in Ministry and Worship* (London: SCM Press, Ltd.).

37. Cf. Ernest W. Southcott, *The Parish Comes Alive* (London: A. R. Mowbray & Company, Ltd., 1956).

38. A reconstruction of an early Christian church, using original frescoes (Dura-Europos), may be seen in the Art Museum of Yale University.

39. See Walter L. Nathan's convincing argument for greater church patronage of contemporary art in *Art and the Message of the Church* (Westminster Studies in Christian Communication, The Westminster Press, 1961), pp. 186–199.

40. See *Liturgical Arts,* a quarterly devoted to the arts in the Roman Catholic Church (Liturgical Arts Society, New York, N.Y.).

41. See the analyses of the Helen Parkhurst *Child's World* records in *Alpark's New Educational Handbook: A Window to the Child's Mind,* ed. by Dorothy R. Luke (Starbridge Publications, 1955).

42. Wilhelm Hahn, *Worship and the Congregation,* p. 40.

◈ ◈ ◈ | # BIBLIOGRAPHY

I. Biblical Background

Cullmann, Oscar, *Early Christian Worship,* tr. by A. Stewart Todd and James B. Torrance (Studies in Biblical Theology, No. 10). Henry Regnery Company, 1953.
—— and Leenhardt, F. J., *Essays on the Lord's Supper.* John Knox Press, 1958.
Delling, Gerhard, *Worship in the New Testament,* tr. by Percy Scott. The Westminster Press, 1962.
Fisher, Fred L., *Prayer in the New Testament.* The Westminster Press, 1964.
Herbert, Arthur S., *Worship in Ancient Israel* (Ecumenical Studies in Worship, No. 5). John Knox Press, 1959.
Higgins, A. J. B., *The Lord's Supper in the New Testament.* Alec R. Allenson, Inc., 1952.
Jeremias, Joachim, *The Eucharistic Words of Jesus,* tr. by Norman Perrin. Charles Scribner's Sons, 1966.
Lamb, John A., *The Psalms in Christian Worship.* London: The Faith Press, 1962.
Moule, C. F. D., *Worship in the New Testament.* John Knox Press, 1962.

II. Historical Background

Brilioth, Yngve T., *Eucharistic Faith and Practice.* London: S.P.C.K., 1953.

Davies, Horton, *Christian Worship: Its History and Meaning.* Abingdon Press, 1957.

────── *The Ecumenical Century, 1900–1965* (Vol. V, *Worship and Theology in England*). Princeton University Press, 1965.

Maxwell, William D., *An Outline of Christian Worship: Its Developments and Forms.* London: Oxford University Press, 1958.

Simpson, Robert L., *The Interpretation of Prayer in the Early Church* (Library of History and Doctrine). The Westminster Press, 1965.

Thompson, Bard (ed.), *Liturgies of the Western Church.* A Living Age Book, Meridian Books, Inc., 1961.

III. LITURGY IN THE ROMAN CATHOLIC TRADITION

Benoît, Jean D., *Liturgical Renewal: Studies in Catholic and Protestant Developments on the Continent,* tr. by Edwin Hudson (Studies in Ministry and Worship, No. 5). London: SCM Press, Ltd., 1958.

Bouyer, Louis, *Life and Liturgy* (University Liturgical Studies, Vol. I). Sheed & Ward, Inc., 1956.

The Church's Worship, Concilium, Vol. 12. The Paulist Press, 1961.

Crichton, John D., *The Church's Worship: Considerations on the Liturgical Constitution of the Second Vatican Council.* Sheed & Ward, Inc., 1964.

Filthaut, Theodor, *Learning to Worship,* tr. by Ronald Walls. The Newman Press, 1966.

Howell, C. (tr.), *The Constitution of the Sacred Liturgy.* Cirencister, 1964.

Jungmann, Josef A., *The Mass of the Roman Rite: Its Origins and Development,* tr. by Francis A. Brunner (2 vols.). Benziger Brothers, Inc., 1951.

Link, Mark J. (ed.), *Faith and Commitment: The Aim of Religious Education* (Loyola Pastoral Studies). Loyola University Press, 1964.

The Liturgy and the Word of God (Papers from the Third National Congress of the Centre de pastorale liturgique, Strasbourg). Liturgical Press.

Reinhold, Hans A., *The Dynamics of the Liturgy*. The Macmillan Company, 1961.
Schillebeeckx, Edward, *Christ: The Sacrament of the Encounter with God*. Sheed & Ward, Inc., 1963.
Sloyan, Gerard S., *Worship in a New Key: What the Council Teaches on the Liturgy*. Herder & Herder, Inc., 1965.

IV. LITURGY IN DENOMINATIONAL TRADITIONS

Brown, Leslie W., *Relevant Liturgy*. Oxford University Press, 1965. (Africa.)
Clark, Neville, *Call to Worship* (Studies in Ministry and Worship). London: SCM Press, Ltd., 1960. (Free Churches.)
Davies, J. G., Cope, G. F., and Tytler, D. A., *An Experimental Liturgy* (Ecumenical Studies in Worship, No. 3). John Knox Press, 1958.
Dobbins, Gaines S., *The Church at Worship*. Broadman Press, 1963. (Southern Baptist.)
Garrett, Thomas S., *Worship in the Church of South India*. John Knox Press, 1958.
Hageman, Howard G., *Pulpit and Table: Some Chapters in the History of Worship in the Reformed Churches*. John Knox Press, 1962.
Hardin, H. G., Quillian, J. D., Jr., and White, J. F., *The Celebration of the Gospel: A Study in Christian Worship*. Abingdon Press, 1964. (Methodist.)
Herrlin, Olle, *Divine Service: Liturgy in Perspective*, tr. by Gene J. Lund. Fortress Press, 1966.
Lehmann, Helmut T. (ed.), *The Meaning and Practice of the Lord's Supper*. Muhlenberg Press, 1961. (Lutheran.)
Macleod, Donald, *Presbyterian Worship: Its Meaning and Method*. John Knox Press, 1965.
Robinson, John A. T., *Liturgy Coming to Life*. The Westminster Press, 1964. (Church of England.)
Schmemann, Alexander, *Sacraments and Orthodoxy*. Herder & Herder, Inc., 1965. (Orthodox.)
Schroeder, Frederick W., *Worship in the Reformed Tradition*. United Church Press, 1966.
Shepherd, Massey H., Jr., *The Liturgical Renewal of the*

Church. Oxford University Press, 1960. (Episcopalian.)
—— *Liturgy and Education.* The Seabury Press, Inc., 1965.
Skogland, John E., *Worship in the Free Churches.* Judson Press, 1965. (Baptist.)
Taylor, Michael J., *The Protestant Liturgical Renewal: A Catholic Viewpoint.* The Newman Press, 1963.
Watkins, Keith, *The Breaking of Bread: An Approach to Worship for the Christian Churches.* The Bethany Press, 1966. (Disciples of Christ.)
Winward, Stephen F., *The Reformation of Our Worship.* John Knox Press, 1965. (British Baptist.)

V. PSYCHOLOGY AND SOCIOLOGY OF WORSHIP

Carrier, Hervé, *The Sociology of Religious Belonging,* tr. by Arthur J. Arrieri. Herder & Herder, Inc., 1965.
Godin, André (ed.), *From Religious Experience to a Religious Attitude.* Loyola University Press, 1965.
Heiler, Friedrich, *Prayer: A Study in the History and Psychology of Religion,* ed. by Samuel McComb and J. Edgar Park. Oxford University Press, 1932.
Lee, Roy S., *Psychology and Worship.* London: SCM Press, Ltd., 1955.
Lenski, Gerhard, *The Religious Factor: A Sociological Study of Religion's Impact on Politics, Economics, and Family Life.* Doubleday & Company, Inc., 1961.
Wach, Joachim, *The Sociology of Religion.* The University of Chicago Press, 1944.
Whitley, Oliver R., *Religious Behavior: Where Sociology and Religion Meet.* Prentice-Hall, Inc., 1964.

VI. THEORY OF WORSHIP

Abba, Raymond, *Principles of Christian Worship.* Oxford University Press, 1957.
Aulén, Gustaf, *Eucharist and Sacrifice,* tr. by Eric H. Wahlstrom. Muhlenberg Press, 1958.
Barth, Karl, *The Knowledge of God and the Service of God,* tr. by J. L. M. Haire and Ian Henderson. London: Hodder & Stoughton, Ltd., 1938.

Dix, Gregory, *The Shape of the Liturgy*. London: The Dacre Press, 1945.

Edwall, Pehr, Hayman, Eric, and Maxwell, William D. (eds.), *Ways of Worship: The Report of a Theological Commission on Faith and Order*. London: SCM Press, Ltd., 1951.

Garrett, Thomas S., *Christian Worship: An Introductory Outline*. London: Oxford University Press, 1961.

Hahn, Wilhelm, *Worship and Congregation*. John Knox Press, 1963.

Hebert, Arthur G., *Liturgy and Society: The Function of the Church in the Modern World*. London: Faber & Faber, Ltd., 1935.

Jasper, R. C. D. (ed.), *The Renewal of Worship*. Oxford University Press, 1965.

Minear, Paul S. (ed.), *Faith and Order Findings* (The Final Report of the Theological Commissions to the Fourth World Conference on Faith and Order, Montreal, 1963). Augsburg Publishing House, 1963.

Nicholls, W., *Jacob's Ladder: The Meaning of Worship*. John Knox Press, 1958.

Phifer, Kenneth G., *A Protestant Case for Liturgical Renewal*. The Westminster Press, 1965.

Seidenspinner, Clarence, *Form and Freedom in Worship* (Minister's Professional Library). Willett, Clark & Company, 1941.

Shands, Alfred, *The Liturgical Movement and the Local Church*, rev. ed. Morehouse-Barlow Co., 1965.

Shepherd, Massey H., Jr., *The Reform of Liturgical Worship: Perspectives and Prospects*. Oxford University Press, 1961.

——— (ed.), *Worship in Scripture and Tradition* (Essays by Members of the Theological Commission on Worship, North American Section, of the Commission on Faith and Order of the World Council of Churches). Oxford University Press, 1963.

Underhill, Evelyn, *Worship*. Harper & Brothers, 1937.

von Allmen, Jean-Jacques, *Worship: Its Theology and Practice*. Oxford University Press, 1965.

Vos, Wiebe, *Worship and the Acts of God*. Nieuwieden: Studia Liturgica Press.

VII. WORD AND PREACHING

Fuller, Reginald H., *What Is Liturgical Preaching?* (Studies in Ministry and Worship, No. 1) Alec R. Allenson, Inc., 1957.

Keir, Thomas H., *The Word in Worship: Preaching and Its Setting in Common Worship.* London: Oxford University Press, 1962.

Lüthi, Walter, and Thurneysen, Eduard, *Preaching, Confession, the Lord's Supper,* tr. by Francis J. Brooke, III. John Knox Press, 1960.

McArthur, Alexander A., *The Christian Year and Lectionary Reform.* London: SCM Press, Ltd., 1958.

Ritschl, Dietrich, *A Theology of Proclamation.* John Knox Press, 1960.

von Allmen, Jean-Jacques, *Preaching and Congregation.* John Knox Press, 1962.

VIII. PRAYER

Daujat, Jean, *Prayer,* tr. by Martin Murphy. Hawthorn Books, Inc., 1964.

Nédoncelle, Maurice, *God's Encounter with Man: A Contemporary Approach to Prayer,* tr. by A. Manson. Sheed & Ward, Inc., 1964.

Phillips, Dewi Z., *The Concept of Prayer.* Schocken Books, Inc., 1966.

von Balthasar, Hans Urs, *Prayer.* Sheed & Ward, Inc., 1961.

IX. SYMBOLS

Davies, J. G., *Holy Week: A Short History.* John Knox Press, 1963.

Denis-Boulet, Nöele M., *The Christian Calendar,* tr. by P. J. Hepburne-Scott. Hawthorn Books, Inc., 1960.

Dobson, H. W., *The Christian Year.* The Macmillan Company, 1963.

Hammond, Peter, *Liturgy and Architecture.* Columbia University Press, 1961.

Horn, Edward T., III, *The Christian Year*. Muhlenberg Press, 1957.

Johnson, F. Ernest (ed.), *Religious Symbolism* (Institute for Religious and Social Studies). Harper & Brothers, 1955.

McArthur, Alexander A., *The Evolution of the Christian Year*. London: SCM Press, Ltd., 1953.

Porter, Harry B., *The Day of Light: The Biblical and Liturgical Meaning of Sunday*. The Seabury Press, Inc., 1960.

Reinhold, H. A., *Liturgy and Art*. Harper & Row, Publishers, Inc., 1966.

Rest, Frederick, *Our Christian Symbols*. Christian Education Press, 1954.

Stowe, Everett M., *Communicating Reality Through Symbols* (Westminster Studies in Christian Communication, ed. by Kendig Brubaker Cully). The Westminster Press, 1966.

X. MUSIC

Northcott, W. C., *Hymns in Christian Worship*. John Knox Press, 1965.

Routley, Erik, *Church Music and Theology*. Muhlenberg Press, 1960.

—— *Hymns Today and Tomorrow*. Abingdon Press, 1964.

—— *Twentieth Century Church Music*. Oxford University Press, 1964.

Wienandt, Elwyn A., *Choral Music of the Church*. The Free Press of Glencoe, Inc., 1965.

XI. CHURCH SCHOOL WORSHIP

Baxter, Edna M., *Learning to Worship*. Judson Press, 1965.

Bowman, Clarice M., *Restoring Worship*, Abingdon-Cokesbury Press, 1951.

Fahs, Sophia L., *Worshipping Together with Questioning Minds*. Beacon Press, Inc., 1965.

Herzel, Catherine, *Helping Children Worship*. Fortress Press, 1963.

Lee, Florence B., *et al.*, *When Children Worship*. Judson Press, 1962.

Vieth, Paul H., *Worship in Christian Education*. United Church Press, 1965.

Williams, John G., *Worship and the Modern Child*. The Macmillan Company, 1957.

INDEX